The Anatomy of Church Leaders

The Anatomy of Church Leaders

Noel G. Clavecilla

RESOURCE *Publications* • Eugene, Oregon

THE ANATOMY OF CHURCH LEADERS

Copyright © 2020 Noel G. Clavecilla. All rights reserved. Except for brief quotations in critical publications or reviews, no part of this book may be reproduced in any manner without prior written permission from the publisher. Write: Permissions, Wipf and Stock Publishers, 199 W. 8th Ave., Suite 3, Eugene, OR 97401.

Resource Publications
An Imprint of Wipf and Stock Publishers
199 W. 8th Ave., Suite 3
Eugene, OR 97401

www.wipfandstock.com

PAPERBACK ISBN: 978-1-7252-7490-7
HARDCOVER ISBN: 978-1-7252-7491-4
EBOOK ISBN: 978-1-7252-7492-1

Manufactured in the U.S.A.   12/04/20

All Scripture quotations are from the Authorized King James Version. Used by permission.

This book is dedicated to all pastors, church workers and church leaders of Christ Our Refuge Bible Christian Church, and to church leaders everywhere who would find this book helpful to their God-given ministry. To my family, Esther, Sam, Mae, Luke Christopher Rebekah, and Jemimah, for their love and support.

Contents

Introduction | ix

1. Church Leaders Are Called by God | 1
    God Calls Leaders | 1
    God Calls the Right Person in the Right Place | 3
    God Calls Leaders to Lead the Church | 5
    God Calls Leaders with Provision for Their Needs | 9
    God Calls Reluctant Leaders | 11

2. Church Leaders Are Grounded on God's Word | 17
    The Leader And the Word of God | 17
    The Leader Must Study the Bible | 18
    The Leader Must Identify False Teachers | 27
    The Leaders Must Protect the Church from False Teachings | 29
    The Leader Must Not Engage in Dispute | 34
    The Leader Must Seek to Maintain Orderliness in the Church | 35
    The Leaders Must Always Seek to Grow Mature in Their Faith | 37

3. Church Leaders Are Prayerful | 38
    Leaders Must Pray for Their Church | 40
    Leaders Must Pray for Other Leaders in the Church | 50
    Leaders Must Pray for All the Members of Their Respective Ministry | 51
    Leaders Must Pray for the Unbelieving Community | 52

4. **Church Leaders are Servants of Christ** | 60
   Servants Are Humble | 61
   Servants Serve the Flock | 65
   Servants Serve Only One Master | 70
   Servants Serve with Gladness of Heart | 70

5. **Church Leaders Are Motivators** | 76
   Motivation by Exhorting through God's Word | 77
   Motivation by Communicating the Goals of Your Church | 80
   Motivation by Personal Dealing | 84

6. **Church Leaders Are Role Models** | 89
   Christ's Example | 89
   Biblical Example | 90
   Secular Example | 92
   Church Example | 98
   Contemporary Example | 103

7. **Church Leaders Are Consultative** | 105
   Consultation by Following Biblical Example | 105
   Consultation by Seeking God's Will | 112
   Consultation by Seeking Advice | 120
   Consultation by Listening to Others' Ideas | 123

8. **Church Leaders Are Respect Earners** | 126
   They Earn Respect Because of Their Labor | 127
   They Earn Respect Because of Their Care | 129
   They Earn Respect Because of Their Admonition | 131

Epilogue | 138

Bibliography | 143

Introduction

IN A SECULAR POINT of view, there is a debate whether leaders are born or made. Those who hold that leaders are born argue that there are people who are naturally-born leaders, especially those who are of the choleric temperament where they are characterized as strong-willed with imposing disposition. On the other hand, those who believe that leaders are made think that even the most timid person can be trained and developed into a leader. While this remains a paradox to some, Christian leadership is entirely different because it is a spiritual gift from God. It is not something you choose, but it is something that God gives to Christians according to His own pleasure. In Rom 12:8, "he that ruleth" (Greek-*proisteimi*) is mentioned, which means "to be over, to superintend, to preside over, to be a protector or guardian."[1] Some are teachers (1 Cor 12:28) that require exercising some form of leadership. In the same verse, the word "government" (Greek-*kuberneisis*) is used which means, "to pilot, to steer, or to direct the church."[2] This is mainly the gift of the local church pastors who understand by heart the mandate of Christ to the church and able to lead the church in the fulfilment of their goals. And of course the gifts of pastor–teacher and evangelist (Eph 4:11).

Not all pastors have the same levels of leadership abilities. Some can effectively lead thirty people, some hundreds, while others by the thousands. Some pastors are great preachers or teachers, some are great evangelists, and some are great in discipleship, while some other pastors are great counselors. Although almost all pastors can function in each of this ministry, but there are varying degrees of effectiveness. Each pastor is designed by God to minister to a specific church at a time, just as each church is unique

1. Thayer, *Thayer's Greek Definitions*.
2. Thayer, *Thayer's Greek Definitions*.

in itself in terms of personality, ministry and composition of people. That's why it is important for a church to consider the strength of a pastor that they are calling while taking into consideration the needs of the church.

Lay leaders are also different from each other in spiritual gifts, through the way they lead and through the way they make their decisions. In the church, there are leaders and there are followers. Truthfully speaking, every Christian is a leader. When Christ said "and teach all nations" (make disciples) (Matt 28:19), He was addressing primarily the disciples, but my view is that He was addressing every believer and the whole church. So whether you're involved in discipleship of a whole church, of a few people or of one person, that makes you a leader. Church leaders are important in the Body of Christ since they do not only represent the whole Body but they also set the pace of how each member should serve. They also play a crucial role in the spiritual growth of each member and the whole church. Although it is God who causes each one to grow, leaders and members must do their part according to God's design of partnership.

In this book we are going to dissect the eight principles or philosophies of church leadership that may be useful to you in your God-given ministry in your local church. Note that all illustrations in this book happened in real life and not fictional. These are firsthand accounts of the author and/or witnessed by very reliable sources.

– 1 –

Church Leaders Are Called by God

> "Paul, a servant of Jesus Christ, called *to be* an apostle,
> separated unto the gospel of God,"
>
> (ROM 1:1)

God Calls Leaders

GOD'S CALLING TO PAUL can be divided into three parts:

1. To a specific character (being a servant)

    A Christian leader is called to function as a servant and not as a boss, manager or supervisor in the church. (This will be dealt with more extensively in Chapter 4 of this book.)

2. To a specific position (to be an apostle)

    Paul was called to be one of the pillars of the church, a very huge responsibility indeed. A church leader is called by God and is spiritually gifted in leading. Although Paul was already a strong leader before he became a Christian, judging by his position in his sect and ability to make an arrest of Christians he found along the way. But he learned that he can never use his charisma to lead the people of God because the disciples were first afraid of him, he was an outsider to them, was not part of the original twelve, and was a murderer for that matter. It took the grace of God for him to be able to win the disciples' trust and to lead in their missionary journeys. Although God used his background to some extent, as well as his religious, social, political, and cultural knowledge to be able to write the majority of the New Testament epistles, Paul never got God's people to listen to him without the aid of the Holy Spirit. Paul had lots of enemies coming from his former religion who were after him, as well as some false teachers. Yet, as God's called servants, the true believers listen to him. And;

3. To a specific ministry (separated unto the gospel of God)

He was called to the ministry of the gospel. The participle "separated" (Greek-*aphoridzow*) which means "to mark off from others by boundaries, to limit,"[1] means that Paul's appointment was to preach the gospel as a travelling evangelist, church planter and guardians of the faith especially to the young Gentile churches. He was separated and limited to the gospel ministry. Although Paul engaged himself to a secular work as a tentmaker, his purpose was to support the ministry. That's why don't judge a pastor if he is involved in a secular job or business without investigating his financial situation. Some may be involved in a pioneering ministry or the church may be too small or poor to provide for the needs of the worker. Pastors work outside to support not only their family but also the ministry. There are some pastors who would pay for their own weekly travelling expenses and the building rentals for their worship hall out of their pockets. Sincere pastors don't work for the money or aren't hirelings.

There was this pastor who was called by a church with only thirty regular members, and after accepting the call, he learned that the church could only support him with a relatively small amount every month. He was allowed to work in an office in an outside company from Monday to Thursday and report for ministry from Friday to Sunday which seemed to be fair for both parties. But soon, the pastor's conviction prevailed and was convinced that he cannot serve God on a part-time basis so he quit the company work and devoted his time fully to the Lord's work. Soon their two children both went to college and the Lord touched the heart of one of their members to hire him as a part-time encoder in a small company to augment his support. After a few years, the church doubled and even almost tripled in membership. But the sad part was that in all those growing years, the church forgot to give him a financial raise. Yet, he did not complain but faithfully does his duty.

1. Thayer, *Thayer's Greek Definitions*.

Therefore church leaders, whether clergy or laity, must remember that they are called to a life of being servants, to their proper place in the ministry, to a life of separation.

God Calls the Right Person in the Right Place

It is sad to think that there are many leaders in the church today who are not supposed to be in their position. Some were appointed or elected because of their popularity, social status or intelligence. Some were placed in their position because they are good speakers; some were due to the fact that they are the leaders of the biggest clan in the church, while some were appointed because nobody is available. Taking into consideration the last note just mentioned, when God wants to start a ministry, He first calls a person to get the work done. So it is better to wait for the right God-appointed leader before starting a ministry in the church. Note the different kinds of leaders:

1. The right person in the right place

    It is assumed that this person has really prayed together with some godly members of the congregation for God's will in his/her ministry. This is ideally good, wherein everyone is happily working with this leader. Although sometimes the majority doesn't agree, remember that the majority is not always right as in the case of the two spies, Joshua and Caleb. There are even times when godly people have conflicting opinion, so it is important for a leader to be fully consecrated to God in full obedience and be given the authority to decide according to God's will. God will open the way for a godly leader and He will always lead the way and make circumstances either favorable or unfavorable for His faithful servant.

2. The right person in the wrong place

    These are the godly leaders placed in the wrong ministry so they become less effective. There are good leaders either wrongly assigned, or lacked in consultation of God's will, or pressured by others. There is this story of a young Christian man who was faithful, available and teachable and was very active in their home church. His typical weekend activities consisted of thoroughly cleaning the chapel on Saturday morning, teaching the choirs in both the mother and daughter churches in the afternoon, and going back to the worship hall at night to clean whatever mess or dirt left by the choir. On a typical Sunday, he would teach the Sunday School class for young people, and would check on the choir for last rehearsal. After the morning service, there would be another choir practice, then he would run again to the daughter church because he had to lead the choir on the afternoon service, followed by another choir practice until early evening. So that is how his regular weekend goes, not mentioning that during weekdays he had to teach and sing with a Christian band in between classes. So when there was an opening for an outreach missionary for a church planting project in an area, he volunteered and packed up his things and embarked on a new journey. At first he was happy knowing that he can focus all his energy and effort on missions alone. But as the years dragged on, he became disillusioned due to several reasons: first, because he had no Bible School or Seminary training for missionary work; secondly, he had no mentor to give him advice; and lastly, the community he was assigned to has only about 1,000 adult members. You can walk around the area in less than two hours, so it has no potential for growth. After 12 years of labor, he was able to gather 30 believers, baptized 9 members, which were later on reduced to just 10 people attending their worship service. Then after prayerful consideration, he decided to dissolve the church. After entrusting the members to some other churches, he accepted the call of another church. If you were his mentor, you might have advised him to go get a seminary degree first and be trained before entering the ministry, to which he did simultaneously while working full time as an outreach missionary. This is an example of having the right person in the wrong place. This story also shows the importance of having a mature and experienced mentor. Although the young pastor considered his experience as part of his training, some mistakes could have been avoided earlier if he was guided properly.

3. The wrong person in the right place

   Sometimes a ministry is doing fine until a wrong leader is placed into position. A certain healthy church was looking for a new pastor and so they formed a search committee. They, however, failed to consult with other pastors within their own group and took the matter in their own hands. A candidate came in, who belongs outside of their group, and they seemed charmed because he had a doctorate degree. They failed to check on what he believed in, and in a couple of years, the church ended up with a heretical doctrine. The leaders of the church fully supported him, and they even succeeded in terminating two other pastors who don't agree with the heresy that they embraced. As a result, the church was divided twice, and the last exodus was a big blow to the church because not only were they many in numbers but most of them were original and second generation members. And lastly:

4. The wrong person in the wrong place

This is totally out of sync and catastrophic. These are the leaders who may be immature and don't know their Bibles, or worse, unregenerate. Some decades ago, an elder of a church slapped the face of their pastor. Some leaders began to dislike this pastor because the members noticed him many times to be drunk with wine when he was on the pulpit. The church itself started with an evangelical teaching and after more than just a decade the church turned liberal. In one Sunday service, they invited priest and nuns to join, and the pastor did not preach the gospel but instead gave all praises to them for their cooperation. At one time, there was a choir concert inside that church, and parts of their repertoires were the songs "Long Haired Lover from Liverpool" by Jimmy Osmond and "Ticket to Ride" by the Beatles. All of their songs in that concert were secular and nothing about Jesus, and part of their hymn singing was the song by Simon and Garfunkel, "Bridge over Troubled Water." This is a case of the wrong person in the wrong place.

God Calls Leaders to Lead the Church

The last two kinds of leader mentioned above can cause a lot of troubles in the church. Some of these leaders actually think that they are better than their pastors and not a few think that they can do the work of a pastor in a more excellent way if they're given the chance. Some think that they can manage the church better, because of their management skills, some think that they can speak better than the pastors in a more oratorical or compelling passion (but take notice of the content of their preaching, it lacks expositional and doctrinal themes and mostly practical application with no doctrinal basis). When the ministry is handed down to lay leaders like these, they begin to mess up. And when problems escalate in the church they begin to point fingers and the pastors are always the ones blamed when actually it was the lay leaders who caused the problems. They won't admit their mistakes and will always label their "weak-willed" (this term is the perception of the problem leaders and not necessarily true) pastors as the culprit, unable to fix things. Some poor pastors are kicked out of the church and labeled as incompetent. One pastor was even terminated of his service in a church, and the following day, he was forced to move out of the pastor's house! What a heartless act by those wrongly-designated leaders!

I have seen some pastors, especially the experienced ones who can see a problem coming out long before it happens. These pastors can anticipate a problem upon the first wrong move of the lay leaders. And most of the time these pastors will give the warning on the first wrong turn but some leaders won't listen, but would eventually give back the helm to the pastor at the slightest sign that the ship is sinking. How blessed are those who heed their warnings, but surely misery will come to those who do not listen because they think that their ideas are better.

Being a New Testament apostle is entirely different from being a Pharisee, like Paul of old. In the same way, being a pastor or a church leader today is far more different from being a manager, CEO or president in a company. The former is called by God while the latter earned his position through hard work.

Let me remind you that the church cannot be run like a private corporation. Let me offer some differences:

1. In the company, employees are paid in order to follow orders that's why you can reprimand them at the slightest mistake, threaten or fire them. This is not applicable in the church because members are all volunteers, and they cannot be forced to do something that they don't like to do. They have to be taught, prayed for, motivated, and not commanded.

2. A private corporation has its own system, rules or guidelines to run the company and any violation can cost a person his job, while the church has the Bible as the source of wisdom to handle the Body of Christ, and you can't just expel anybody for neglecting their church duties. That's why pastors spend much time in studying the Holy Scriptures. But study time is limited by other unnecessary concerns in the church. The pastor is expected to conduct Bible studies, visit and in some cases, evangelize. In some churches, if there is no addition in church membership by the end of the year, the pastor is sometimes blamed for being lazy or not doing his part in the Great Commission. But take this simple analogy: The shepherd's work is to feed and

take care of the sheep, and once the sheep grow healthy and strong, they are the ones who give birth and multiply. In the same way, the ministry of the pastor is to teach the Word, pray for each member and administer the church. Once the members are trained, through the modeling of the pastor, they should be involved in other ministries in accordance to their spiritual gifts, including evangelism and spiritual multiplication. Now if you are a lay person who thinks that you know the Bible too well that you can teach better than your pastor, let me tell you this, "You know nothing at all!" Because in my experience I can tell that those disciples that are growing in their faith and have been believers for decades readily admit that the more they study the Word, the more they realize that they know nothing at all.

An 87-year-old retired Pastor always had a pen, notebook and a book with him wherever he went. One day, he was talking to a young pastor who was in his early 20's, sharing what he has just read with excitement as though it was the first time he learned about it. The young man thought to himself, "What's so exciting about it? I've known that for a couple of years already." Obviously, the young man doesn't know where the old man was coming from. Now, that young man is approaching 60 years of age, and he is now acting the same way the old man did several decades ago: always getting excited for what he discovers each day from the Word of God. Because the more mature you get, the more you see God in His holiness and grace for saving a wretched person like you, and the more you discover that you know nothing at all.

3. In the secular firm, the establishment only cares for the employee as long as he/she's useful or productive but will dispose him/her as soon as performance goes down. The enterprise will not waste their resources on under-performing or non-performing assets. But in the church, people give financial support instead of receiving salary, so the church can minister to the elderly, the orphans, widows and those who are sick. The church loves every soul that they come across with, and will listen, care and welcome people, even those who are unproductive by worldly standard.

4. Companies set targets for sales and production. But in the church, you cannot set a goal of how many would be saved by the end of the year because saving people all depends on God while our main responsibility is to preach the gospel. This is a common mistake by some

churches. One pastor made several pages of feasibility study about the growth of their church. It was a complete study, which included even the ratio of probability of those who would accept and reject the gospel. He predicted that after four years there will be 500 members in their church. But after four years, membership of the church was reduced from almost one hundred to twenty five members! In setting goals for the church, you must not set the desired results, but set your goal in what you can do.

Here is a simple test in goal setting, and try to select the right answer:

a. By the end of the year, there will be fifty souls evangelized and added to the church.
b. By the end of each week, each member of the evangelism team will witness to at least a single soul.
c. After six months, there'll be ten new Bible Study leaders in the church.
d. To be able to train twenty prospective Bible Study leaders in the church for the next 6 months.

The first goal (a) as we said above is defective, because nobody can predict how many souls can be saved even if you go all-out in your evangelistic efforts or even rent a football stadium and create a fantastic program. These will not guarantee of even a single convert because saving people is entirely the work of God. It's beyond your control.

The second goal (b) is achievable because you know how many people are in your evangelism team who can go out at least once a week or during weekends. This shows that you are not pre-occupied with how many souls will be saved because it all depends on God, but you are concerned with souls and on what you can do which is within your control.

The third goal (c) is possible if you plan to train fifty people with 80 percent dropout rate leaving you with ten new Bible Study leaders. But the problem is you'll never know how many will continue and finish the course and how many will drop out. It is a fact that some people will finish the course for the sake of just completing it. Of those who finished, you'll never know how many will be effective Bible Study leaders or how many will have the patience to last.

The fourth goal, (d) just like the second goal (b) is feasible because it focuses on what you can do and not the result.

So setting goal is not a numbers game, which is beyond your control. It's more of what you can do. Just commit to God what you have, use it and let God cause the growth. Having said the above, I implore all church leaders, board members, deacons or any lay leaders to halt from making decisions or treating the church ministries using a worldly point of view. Please always consult your pastors for guidance and always respect his decisions unless he goes beyond Scriptural principles. Besides, if there is someone in the church who better understands the ministry and has the heart for it, it is your pastor and he is the one whom God makes accountable for the whole church.

God Calls Leaders with Provision for Their Needs

When God calls leaders, He empowers them with the appropriate spiritual gifts used in the power of the Holy Spirit. He will not call you to head the evangelism ministry if you don't have the gift of evangelism lest the ministry will end up in confusion. Or be a Sunday School teacher if you cannot teach. Worse, to be a Pastor if you don't have the gift of teaching and leading.

Not only will God provide you with empowerment, but your financial needs as well. This is not only true with pastor, missionaries and full time workers but also to all lay leaders who have weekday jobs. Think of your God-given work as part of your ministry to support not only your needs and that of your family, but also the work of God. Remember that it is God who provides all your needs, therefore use all your resources for His glory. Just an old wise pastor once told his children who were blessed financially, "Remember children, the reason why God has blessed you financially is for you to help the workers of God who have less." I don't say that you don't save a part of your income or spend it for a good holiday vacation and give all to the ministry, but what I am saying is that you must be wise in spending your hard-earned money. You can eat in an expensive restaurant but do it in special occasions only. You can go out shopping but please make a list of all the things that you need and not what you just want. The extra money you save can do a lot in the ministry.

Here is some reality check: In my many years in the ministry, I have seen dedicated pastors, missionaries or church workers who labor hard in the Lord's vineyard without receiving anything. There are some pastors who preach on Sunday morning and come home without food on their table to feed their families on lunch time while their members are enjoying their meals at the same time. There are some workers who send their children to school without eating their breakfast and come home later in the afternoon asking for food, but there's still none to feed them. Do you know what's heartbreaking for a pastor? It is when your children ask for food and you can't give an answer because there is none.

    You may reason out that it's a part of their trials so that they can easily empathize with others who are in need, and they need to strengthen their faith. While that is very much true but do you know how it feels to teach or preach with empty stomach? As one pastor said, "The money of the pastor or Christian worker is sometimes still in the pocket of some members." Some missionaries whom we send overseas are depending of course to God for provision, but God wants to use us back home as we make pledges to support them either individually or as a church. We pledge our prayers and financial support. Sometimes we are good on our promises on the first few months or years, but being away for a long time makes the missionary unpopular back at home so our prayers and financial support dwindle gradually. Even when the missionary is faithful in their report we tend to lose interest in them. And when the home church is experiencing financial difficulties the first thing they do is to cut off the support of the missionary. As one pastor asked his congregation hypothetically, "Who wants to trade places with our missionaries? You will be sent out to the field and the missionaries will come home and support you instead." Of course that won't happen but the pastor would like to stress how hard it is to be on the frontline, and we at home should not forget our responsibilities to them.

    I'm not saying that you make a survey of all the workers and try to help each of them. But you can zero in on a single or group of workers (depending on how much God gives you), and be a blessing to them. There is this Christian man who, after receiving his monthly pay check, pays all the bills, and still finds extra money in His wallet, would wonder and ask himself, "Who needs help right now?" And most of the time, a day won't pass without someone knocking at his door, whether it be a brother or sister, or a pastor from another church who needs help. When God fills our cup, it is meant to be shared with others.

Church Leaders Are Called by God

God Calls Reluctant Leaders

In the Bible, you have read that there were men who were readily available to heed God's call just like Abraham, Samuel and Isaiah. But there were also those who were hesitant like Jonah and Moses. You may have heard of testimonies of some pastors who heard God's call but were reluctant at first, and some have attempted to escape but God pursued and overtook them. Let's look back at the story of Moses on how he tried to evade God's call.

And so it happened one day after forty years of tending his father-in-law's flock in a solitary mode that God began to speak to reveal His plan to Him. Moses might have thought, "What a way to spend the rest of my life here!" It was so peaceful, with a family of his own and away from the gruesome sights of slaves being whipped and forced to do unbearable labor. Best of all, he was away from those who threaten his life. He seemed to enjoy this kind of life more than what God called him to do, and that was to lead Israel out of bondage from Egypt, as revealed by his excuses.

Now let us look to some of His excuses:

1. The first excuse: "Who *am* I?" (Exod 3:11)

    God's response: "Certainly I will be with thee" (Exod 3:12) God made it clear to him His plan of rescuing the Israelites from bondage and of them having a permanent residence in the Promised Land. Maybe Moses liked the idea as he listened to God, since his siblings were left in Egypt. But when God dropped the bomb and told him that it was he whom He was calling to lead Israel out of Egypt, he was caught off guard! So Moses replied in v.11, "Who *am* I, that I should go unto Pharaoh, and that I should bring forth the children of Israel out of Egypt?" If we can only hear the intonation of Moses' voice, we can easily tell if he said that out of humility or out of fear. God's reply in v.12 was, "Certainly I will be with thee" which is an assurance of His divine accompaniment. If Moses said it out of humility, then what he meant was he was just a lowly shepherd, so how can Pharaoh listen to him as well as all the Israelites? Although he was once a prince of Egypt, that was four decades ago and he was long forgotten. Then God assured him that they will respect and listen to him because of the Lord's presence in his life. If it is out of fear, then it is grounded on what happened forty years ago when he killed an Egyptian, and Pharaoh hunted to kill him. Then God assured him of His protection and preservation of his life. The second interpretation is the more likely one because in Exod 4:19, God told him, "Go, return into Egypt: for all the men are dead which sought thy life." God knows Moses' reluctance to go back so He told him this. This will become clearer after we looked at his fifth and last excuse. If this is the case, then he feigned his "Who am I?" humility as an excuse. Based on experience of some pastors, it is best to call leaders who are reluctant because of their genuine humility. But you must be very discerning because there are also those who pretend to be humble and will initially say no but have hidden agendas. They might say no initially because of false humility or they might just want to feel important and need to be called at least twice. Don't commit the mistake of calling these kinds of people without knowing that God called them first.

2. The second excuse: "What *is* his name? What shall I say unto them?" (Exod 3:13b)

    God's response: "I AM THAT I AM: I AM hath sent me unto you." (Exod 3:14)

    Never in the hundreds of years of slavery in Egypt and the forty years of wandering did the Israelites ask God's name. He was always introduced this way, especially when the names of the first early three forefathers were associated with it. Assuming that Moses did not know that, still God didn't give him a specific name but instead introduced Himself as "I AM, THAT I AM." (v.14). We will not go deeper in the meaning of this name, but God wants Moses to understand that He is the ever present God, and in v.15, He repeated His introduction to Moses from v.6 about Who He is. He meant that He is the same God who existed and called Abraham, Isaac and Jacob and the same God during that time and forever. God did not give Moses a long lecture about Himself, but simply told him that He is the One whom his forefathers believed in. While it is normal for anyone to know who is sending them, still, this did not satisfy Moses so he continued with his excuses.

3. The third excuse: "But, behold, they will not believe me, nor hearken unto my voice" (Exod 4:1)

    God's response: "What *is* that in thine hand?" (Exod 4:2)

    After God repeated His call to Moses, and after telling him what will transpire in Egypt which included the initial rejection by the King of Egypt and the bountiful provision of those coming out, his apprehension still increased and he made this third excuse. We don't know for sure what was running in the mind of Moses. We can only assume that perhaps he was regretting his curiosity of coming near the burning bush or he was thinking of finding a way to end this conversation. Perhaps he was just stalling. The Lord answered him by displaying two miracles: the first was the staff becoming a snake and Moses was so terrified that he ran away from it, and the second was his hand becoming leprous. Although his reaction was not written, we can further assume that he was also terrified. We can also learn from God's response to him that God can do something great in what you possess. He can turn your weakness into strength. He can move people with your spiritual small prayers. And you might think that the small amount you give in the offering plate or basket will not make a difference at all, but once you give it to God cheerfully, then He can use it to save souls. Then God told a third miracle that will about to take place upon reaching Egypt (Exod 4:9), that is the water from the Nile to become blood. It was at this moment that Moses stated his next excuse.

4. The fourth excuse: "I *am* not eloquent" (Exod 4:10)

    God's response: "Who hath made man's mouth?" (Exod 4:11)

    Moses had a speech impediment. He said he was slow of speech and tongue and he could not properly bring out a word. We don't know exactly what kind of speech defect he had or what exactly he meant by that but I can offer some suggestions:

- His prolonged silence as shepherd for forty years could have affected his speech. Try not using one of your arms for five years and it will surely shrink.

- He may not be familiar with the Hebrew language and may have forgotten the Egyptian language. A person who speaks any language or dialect fluently and does not practice it for conversation for a longer period of time may have the tendency to forget some words, although to some individuals it may not be true. Just like in a segment in "Thank you Philippines (Part 1/2)" that was featured in YouTube Channel in 2015 where an elderly Jewish man who lived in the Philippines during and after World War 2 left to live in Israel, and having been away for more than 60 years, he still could speak the Filipino language fluently. He did not forget the local dialect considering that he stayed in the Philippines for only about 10 years.[2] Moses, however, stayed in the palace for 40 years and his first word spoken was probably Egyptian, so it's hard to believe that he had forgotten at all.

- He might have this speech defect since his Egyptian days with the phrase "either in the past." In Acts 7:22 it was said "And Moses was learned in all the wisdom of the Egyptians, and was mighty in words and in deeds." This verse might mean that he had speech defect but still can communicate well while in Egypt and that God enabled him to speak clearly or that Aaron became his mouthpiece upon returning in Egypt, because the Lord said to him in verses 11 and 12, "Who has made man's mouth? Who makes him mute, or deaf, or seeing, or blind? Is it not I, the LORD?" Now therefore go, and I will be with thy mouth, and teach thee what thou shalt say." (Exod 4:11,12)

- But after his first try of confronting Pharaoh, he was rejected and the people blamed him. He then said to the Lord, "Behold, the people of Israel have not listened to me. How then will Pharaoh listen to me, for I am of uncircumcised lips?" (Exod 6:12). Moses' fear has happened: the rejection of the people. However, the Lord answered him by giving him the assurance that He will enable him to deliver His message. Then when Moses saw all his excuses were overruled by God, he became very honest with God with his last excuse.

5. The fifth excuse: "O my Lord, send, I pray thee, by the hand *of him whom* thou wilt send." (Exod 4:13)

    God's response: "And the anger of the LORD was kindled against Moses," (Exod 4:14)

    To paraphrase it in today's language, God was conveying to him, (although God did not say these exact words but just to get the essence of the meaning) "Enough Moses with your nonsense reasoning! Your brother Aaron will meet you and he will be your mouth as he will speak for you. End of arguments!" Actually, this was the first thing that Moses wanted to tell God at the beginning of their discourse so he was trying to reason out and tried to make a way out. There may be multiple reasons for his reluctance but the main reason we could see is because he feared for his life. So when Moses was prepared to

2. IsraelinPH, "Thank You Philippines (Part1/2)."

Church Leaders Are Called by God

leave Midian, God told him the good news, "Go, return to Egypt: for all the men are dead which sought thy life." (Exod 4:19). Why didn't God say it at the beginning of their dialogue? Well, God already knew Moses' greatest fear so it was for the sake of Moses to discover his hidden fear that kept him away from people for the last forty years of his existence. This was the last assurance of the Lord as he was preparing to leave Midian. Notice that God saved this information for last which should have been the first thing that God told him in order to extract an immediate response from Moses. But this information was later on exposed for it was actually for Moses to discover his own fear. Moses might have contemplated his fear during his forty years of solitude but it will never come to full realization unless it will be put to test. So when he ran out of excuses he frankly told God, "Please have someone else to go and not me." We can learn from this event that when God calls a leader, He prepares him and removes all hindrances by equipping him and paving the way. God has trained Moses as prince for forty years and as shepherd for another forty years. Being a prince has enabled Moses to become familiar with the palace and be knowledgeable on how to gain access to Pharaoh. He knew the right people to talk to or perhaps some elderly Egyptians of his time still recognized him. We don't know the protocol in the palace that time, but under normal circumstances a Hebrew with the status of being a slave can't seek an audience with a Pharaoh. But God used Moses' long history of being a prince to pull that one out. By being a shepherd, Moses learned patience in taking care of their sheep as he will soon take care of God's stiff-necked people for forty years in the wilderness. Although tending sheep for the same duration of time was far easier because they don't complain, than leading people who was always whining about their condition.

Why did God call Moses although he didn't want to go? God can call anybody according to His good pleasure and not according to any person's ability, intelligence or social status. He knew even before birth whom He's going to call that's why He prepared that person from birth so no one can escape His call. Our background from childhood to adulthood is not the reason why God calls us as leaders, but He shapes our past experiences so that we can be the kind of leaders that He wants us to be.

If you are not called to be a leader, don't force yourself into it and out of modesty wait to be asked because you may become an instrument for destroying the fellowship. This is not only true for lay members but for pastors as well. During a ministerial fellowship election of officers, a certain pastor desperately wanted to become the president so he told the other pastor sitting beside him, "If no one nominates me, nominate me!" He was nominated but did not win and another pastor was elected. After the other pastor's term was over he somehow managed to be elected as President, and it was during his term that the fellowship has almost dissolved.

Some churches call pastors because of their impressive track records, such as multiple ministries and broad experience in pastoring churches. However, having pastored many churches could sometimes be a sign that the pastor would most likely not stay long in a church due to lack of focus, unless that pastor is an evangelist or a church planter. Others call a pastor because of his Masters or Doctorate degree without even checking the seminary background or doctrines. The result of this would most likely a church with false doctrines. Also, some lay leaders are assigned or appointed in a ministry based on their talents or acquired knowledge, and not on their character or spiritual gifts. In our church, Christ Our Refuge Bible Christian Church, we stated this in our guidelines: "Character is more important than gifting." We highly value godly character in our leaders. A leader can be trained in the ministry and eventually improve in the area of gifting, but there is no school that can produce a holy living and righteous lifestyle.

Leaders are called by God, and He provides the necessary spiritual gift for them so that they can be effective and eventually give God all the glory for successes in the ministry.

– 2 –

Church Leaders Are Grounded on God's Word

> "This book of the law shall not depart out of thy mouth; but thou shalt meditate therein day and night, that thou mayest observe to do according to all that is written therein: for then thou shalt make thy way prosperous, and then thou shalt have good success."
>
> (JOSH 1:8)

The Leader And the Word of God

WE CAN LEARN FROM this Old Testament lesson and apply it to the church leaders of today. To be the successor of Moses was a tall order for Joshua. He needed guidance that directly came from God so the Lord spoke to him (Josh 1:1–9) and promised him the land that He will give to His people. He also instructed him to be strong and very courageous because He will be with him all throughout his campaign as He was with Moses. Then in v.8, The Lord reminded Him of the importance of clinging to His Words to guarantee claiming of the Promised Land. The words "prosperous" and "good success" are interpreted by some preachers and teachers today as being financially blessed and becoming successful in careers, but these interpretations are out of context. These have nothing to do with material wealth or career advancement, but for the Jewish people's success in conquering the land given to them. The Promised Land was occupied by other inhabitants and they had to drive them away and engage them in war in order to claim the land.

Conquering Jericho was a tough job for Joshua and his men. It was surrounded by fortified walls. This was what the Israelites faced as they marched around the city daily for seven days. So it was impossible for the Israelites to penetrate the fortress of Jericho.

Objectively speaking, any attacker will be killed by flying arrows from the high fortress before coming near the gates of the wall. They even needed a trebuchet to hurl big objects that will at least penetrate the thick wall but it was not yet invented that time. And Joshua, being a war tactician, knew that there was no way that they can win that war unless God intervenes. Forty years ago he was a part of the original twelve spies (Num 13:1—14:45) that were sent to Canaan, and the ten spies lost heart but Joshua and Caleb remained firm that they can overcome because the Lord can bring them into the land. That's why he learned to rely on God's every instruction all throughout the crusade. The Lord spoke to Joshua at least six times before the battle in Jericho (3:7; 4:1,15; 5:2; 5:13–15; 6:2). He gave him step-by-step instructions on what to do instead of just giving one generic coaching. There was even a break in the Lord's communing with him, in 5:13–15, the Captain of the Lord of Host appeared to him assuring him that God was with them in their battle.

Although scholars were divided in the identity of this Captain, because some believe that it was the pre-incarnate Christ by the worship He received from Joshua,[1] while others believe that the Captain was a superior angelic being[2] as shown in how Joshua called him "Lord" (Hebrew-*adonai*)[3] with the English equivalent of "Master," and prostrating oneself is part of the culture in the ancient times. But the message is clear, that the battle is the Lord's, and He will make the impossible possible. Joshua and his army were not alone in this battle but he had the heavenly host not as a back-up but at the forefront of the battle.

The Leader Must Study the Bible

Leaders should always consult with God to ensure that they are doing His will. In the previous chapter, we discussed about leaders being called by

---

1. Gill, *John Gill's Exposition of the Entire Bible.*
2. Fredreich and Delitzsch, *Keil and Delitzsch Commentary on the Old Testament.*
3. Brown et al., *Brown-Driver-Briggs' Hebrew Definition.*

Church Leaders Are Grounded on God's Word

God, and we now add that God speaks through the Bible to any leader He chose. Church leaders should be grounded in the Word of God and use it as guide to administering the affairs of the church. There should be an absolute norm for everyone to follow or else there will be chaos and endless debate in the church. It is a must for all church leaders to have their daily devotion in the Word and prayer, and have personal time to study the Bible. In this modern age of technology there are many Bible applications such as different Bible translations, Hebrew and Greek dictionaries, Bible Atlas and sound commentaries that can be downloaded in cellular phones, tablets or laptops. You can bring it anywhere and study while waiting for your transportation or during your free time. This is unlike the old times when you have to go to the library or buy all the books, have a big office table and chair, where you sit and study. But times have changed. You can't bring a big and thick Strong's Exhaustive Concordance and two big Study Bibles all the time with you. A certain downloadable application contains more than forty different Bible Translations and twenty-five different Bible Dictionaries, so there's no excuse for any Christian leader not to study. There are five modes in the intake of the Word of God in your lives (adopted from The Word Hand illustration by The Navigators):

1. Hearing of the Word

    Listen to all preaching and teaching services of your church and don't choose only the preacher or teacher that you like. Remember that whoever is standing behind the pulpit to preach, God is speaking, therefore you must listen. Be sure to have your Bible open before you and just like the Bereans in Paul's time, examine for yourself if what is being preached is truthful. You can listen through your car radio or through the internet. You can ask your pastor if you don't know the preacher, and determine if he is worth your listening time.

2. Reading of the Word

    It is imperative that each leader must read the whole Bible from Genesis to Revelation in order to better understand and have a right concept of who God is, and get a glimpse of His whole perfect will and plan. Some might complain that they can't understand many parts of the Bible and get bored when they get to the part of the long list of genealogies. First of all, you must know that almost everyone I know who reads the Bible for the first time share the same sentiment to me, well God knew that even before He created anything so He moved the early church fathers to arrange the sequence of the Bible not according to the date each book was written but by grouping them together. You will notice that the first seventeen books in the Old Testament were written in a narrative fashion so you can read the Bible historically like a novel. The next part is a compilation of five poetical books, followed by seventeen books written by different prophets. You will not understand the poetry or prophetic parts of the Old Testament if you did not read first the historical part. The same is true with the compilation of the New Testament books beginning with five narratives followed by twenty-one letters written by some of the Apostles to churches and some individuals and then the end times, the Book of Revelation. God knows that humans like to read stories first because we are imaginative beings who can understand better if we can picture in our minds what's going on and can empathize with the feelings of the Biblical characters that we're reading. Just plain reading of the Bible is actually enjoyable because it is complete with different genres of stories. It has action, drama, suspense, love stories, some are humorous and some can make you cry. I would always end up in tears every time I read the story of Rahab, the prostitute from Jericho who was saved from the God-led Israelite invasion of their fortress because she hid the Israelite spies. She was incorporated into the Israelite society, introduced to the One True God and later on married to one of the men in her new country. Never in her wildest dream that someday a man would truly love and respect her and have her own family. Because just years before, she was an outcast in her society, detested especially by the wives of the men whom she had an affair with. If you stretch some more of your imagination, (although it is not inspired so don't preach this as part of the Scripture), perhaps some of the wives of husbands she had an affair with, would have cursed her, spat on her and worse, might have even stoned her every time she passed by walking down the street. To them, she was a home wrecker seducing their husbands with their hard-earned money. Who would have thought that one day she would become one of the revered grand matriarchs of Kings and eventually of our Lord Jesus Christ? Now isn't that a great story?

    To enjoy reading the Bible you must have a good English translation of it (the King James Version is not recommended for reading unless you're familiar with the grammatical structure of this version). You can opt to use a Bible that is translated into your first language or

Church Leaders Are Grounded on God's Word

dialect. If you can't understand some parts, just keep on reading and mark that section for future study. Read even the long list of names. At first, you might find them insignificant, but as you grow deeper in the Word you will find that some names listed will play important roles later on. So set a plan and a goal to finish reading the whole Bible. Having made a mathematical calculation, I estimated that you can finish reading it in a year if you read three chapters from the Old Testament in the morning and one chapter from the New Testament in the evening. Or two chapters every day and you're done in two years. If you plan to read one chapter a day you may have gone through it in 3 years and 4 months. So begin reading now and don't wait for the start of the year.

3. Studying of the Word

It is not enough to hear and read the Word. A leader must also set aside a time to diligently study God's Word. Since the Bible was written in different languages by actual people to actual recipients who lived in another country, culture, and time, it is necessary to study to get the proper interpretation. The interpreter must be able to know the original intention of each author based on his cultural, geographical and social background as well as the background of the original recipient. You will need tools in your study like several Bible translations, pen, notebook, marker, Hebrew and Greek dictionary or concordance, Bible Atlas, Bible Customs and Traditions, Study Bible and Bible Commentaries. Whether you're using actual books or electronic gadgets like tablet or laptop, you will be needing all of the above. Here are some general tips especially for those leaders who haven't had the experience of a serious study of the Bible:

a. Set aside a regular weekly time and place for your study. Set aside a minimum of 2 hours a week and choose a private place free from distraction as possible, with all your study tools.

b. Pray. Pray for the Holy Spirit to open your heart and mind and to guide you in your inquiry.

c. Choose a book, a chapter, verse or verses to study.

d. Using a Study Bible or the internet, learn about the author's background, the recipient, the theme and outline of the book.

e. Read first the whole book several times until you become familiar with the flow of thoughts.

f. You can follow these 3 simple steps:
   - Observation

     List all your observations, important words, time sequences, repetitive words, customs and traditions, key verses and some difficult passages. Use your Hebrew or Greek dictionaries to determine the original meaning of words.

   - Interpretation

     The rule in interpreting a passage is to interpret a verse according to the context of the whole book and according to the teachings of the whole Bible. To understand a single verse, read the verses before and after the verse you are interpreting, or the preceding and succeeding chapters, or the Book from where you get the verse. Try to look for cross references if your Bible has footnotes for these. These are the verses from other books of the Bible which may shed light on your study. If you still can't find the right meaning, try asking your pastor or a mature believer. Don't be discouraged if no one can give you a satisfying answer because there are really parts of Scriptures that even Bible Scholars differ in views. But please don't attempt to give your own ideas in it and build a new doctrine out of an obscure passage because this is how cults fall.

   - Application

     Remember that correct interpretation leads to correct application. You can begin by asking yourself what have you learned about God the Father, Son or the Holy Spirit? What have you learned about the human nature and the Christian life? About the church and Christian Service?

   Then follow these four common steps that have been handed to us: S-ins to forsake; P-romises to claim; E-xamples to follow; and C-ommands to obey.

g. After you're done with your study, you may consult good commentaries for comparison of your own work and additional insights. Remember that commentaries are made by humans too. Some commentators will agree on major doctrines, but may vary in explaining minor issues. But before you choose your stand on an interpretation on minor teachings, be sure that you make a thorough study on it. Please don't be dogmatic about it, because someday, you may or may not find yourself shifting to another position. So on essential issues, agree with your church's doctrine. On minor teachings, you must subscribe to what your church generally believes in. You are entitled to your own opinion but never teach it publicly. Remember that we have an outside enemy waiting on the sideline to turn a minor issue into a major one that might be catastrophic and will result to a divided church.

h. Lastly, write down all your studies and keep it. You will always find it helpful someday if you're asked to teach the Bible.

4. Meditating of the Word

After studying the Word, the next thing to do is to practice it and meditate upon it. Weigh the matters in your heart and give your thoughts in it. Meditating is like masticating or chewing the food in your mouth. You should chew your food very well before swallowing, not only for proper digestion but to get more energy from the food you eat. As you meditate on God's word, you get spiritual nourishment from it. The Apostle Paul told the Philippian believers in Philippians 4:8,9a, "Finally, brethren, whatsoever things are true, whatsoever things *are* honest, whatsoever things *are* just, whatsoever things *are* pure, whatsoever things *are* lovely, whatsoever things *are* of good report; if *there be* any virtue, and if *there be* any praise, think on these things. Those things, which ye have both learned, and received, and heard, and seen in me, do:" He gave eight things where we should focus our minds into. The commands "think" which means "to meditate on," and "do" which means "to practice," are both in the present tense. The Greek present tense suggests continuity, so they literally mean, "keep on thinking or keep on meditating" and "keep on doing or keep on practicing." To meditate day and night does not only suggest a specific time in the morning and night, but a whole day affair. Every time you get a break from your daily work and activity, you must ponder upon His Word. So instead of thinking about nonsense things whenever there is a lull in your mind, try meditating on His Word.

5. Memorizing of the Word

One prerequisite in your meditation is committing in memory a verse or verses from the Bible. The Word of God is symbolized as, and compared to a sword (Eph 6:17; Heb 4:12), an offensive weapon which Roman soldiers always carry whenever they go out to protect themselves against any aggressor. In the same way, we have an unseen enemy: a roaming and roaring lion ready to attack us during our unguarded moments. His greatest weapons in his arsenal are his lies and deception. We can't fight him squarely with our own strength, that's why the Sword of the Spirit was given to us to ward off any of his advances. It is the same Sword that Christ used to drive him away when He was tempted in the wilderness (Matt 4:1–11). Some elderly Christians make it an excuse that they are unable to memorize because they are already suffering from memory loss. While this is true to some, it is not a valid excuse for a person who doesn't suffer from any memory problem. That's why we encourage younger people to memorize as many verses as they can. Because as they grow older and begin to suffer memory loss, the first to be forgotten are the more recent memories while older memories are retained.

A young Christian guy was always whispering to himself and when he was asked about it, he humbly said that he was memorizing the Book of Philippians and that he was halfway through. This was wise on his part because as he grows older he may forget some parts of the book but there are lots of verses that will be retained in his memory. As we said above older people may forget the more recent memories while older memories are retained. A 90-year-old pastor was being interviewed by his grandson about their family tree, and he began reciting the name of his grandparents, parents, siblings and their spouses, with some details on how they died and where they were buried. Then he moved on to his nine children and their spouses and the names of some older grandchildren. But when he came to name the youngest son's wife whom he was living with that time, he paused for a minute and asked, "What is the name of his wife?" He totally can't recall the name of a person whom he sees every day. Perhaps you've heard stories of elderly people who can't find where they placed their eye glasses because they are wearing it or some dying people who can't recognize the loved ones who surround them, and begin calling the names of dead people. Others find this creepy, thinking that they are actually seeing the ghost of the departed ones, while others dismiss this as pure hallucination. Well, neither of the two mentioned are correct because it's just how the brain works. The most recent memories

Church Leaders Are Grounded on God's Word

are the first ones lost and the older memories are retained or slowly fade out. That's why some older people can vividly narrate important events that took place sixty to seventy years ago, but may not be able to recall the things that happened the day before.

Several decades ago, a story was told in a devotional booklet about a dying man who was suffering from a great memory loss, and who was surrounded by his family and their pastor. One by one, the family members approached him, from his wife to all his children, but he could not recognize any one in the room. He was confused, and wondered who these people were and what were they doing in his room. Finally, after a moment of silence, the pastor asked him, "Do you know Jesus Christ?" His eyes suddenly brightened up and with a smile on his face, he replied, "Yes, I know Him, He is my Lord and Savior!"

So while you're still young and sharp, begin to memorize verses, a whole chapter and if possible, a whole book in the Bible, so that there will be a lot stored in your memory as you grow old. Perhaps you've heard stories of some people who were converted in the faith and how they've recalled Bible verses that they've learned in Sunday School when they were still young.

Although God doesn't speak through our leaders in audible voice anymore so His will sometimes is not specified, the Written Revelation's principles are clear. That's why it is the duty of our pastors to rightly exegete the Bible and provide us with the proper interpretation and application. Note also that all pastors have the gift of preaching and teaching, but each pastor is gifted differently on how they exercise this gift. That's why we have pure theologians and pure preachers and teachers. God has given true pastors different abilities and intelligence in handling the Word. But I do not say it as an excuse for pastors with "lesser abilities or intelligence" (I don't mean to say it in a derogatory fashion) not to study hard. They must have at least a general knowledge of every doctrine in the Bible.

Some might argue that all pastors should be diligent in the study of the Word in order for them to have the same views rather than different interpretations. That's ideally correct but realistically and historically speaking, it doesn't happen that way because there are both godly and intelligent men in different school of thoughts. And we can't understand why God allows it to happen that way. (We're speaking in the context of Bible vs. Bible views and not Bible vs. heretical or cultic views). There is also the difference in intellectual capacity. It is a general knowledge that not all people have the same IQs. And so it is true with pastors. Why didn't God give every pastor the same level of intelligence? My theory is that because God designed each of them to a specific church where they are to serve. You cannot expect a natural-born tribal pastor to read all the works of Matthew Henry, the historical writings of Josephus or memorize all the endings of Greek nouns and verbs so that they can teach their congregation. In the same way, a highly-intellectual pastor may not be able to understand how a simple mind works. There was a candidate for baptism who failed the interview conducted by two church workers who have some amount of theological training because he wasn't able to give the desired answer and was referred back to the pastor for further Bible study. It was in that study that the pastor learned something, that there are some believers who know their doctrine, but are unable to articulate it. So the pastor just recommended the candidate to be baptized without subjecting him to another interview by the two leaders because most likely he will fail again.

A respected seminary who allowed a student to graduate even though he failed his final examinations on two major subjects is to be admired. The reason was clear and I say: "Should you prevent a student from graduating to become a pastor when there is evidence that he is called by God?" This could be a dilemma to some seminaries who maintain a certain scholastic level. But how did the seminary know that he was truly called by God? Well, that student displayed good character during his stay at the seminary, and every day after his classes, he will go to work in the evening to support his studies which made him unable to go to the library and study. Aside from this, he has proven that he is not a no-brainer at all when he passed his final oral examination with flying colors to which one of the faculty members commented, "He could teach in a Bible School." Obviously some pastors may not be good in memorizing names of some church fathers or dates and places in church history but what is important is that they could come out with a sound interpretation of the Bible so that they could feed the flock of God under their care.

Meanwhile, a pastor was invited to preach in the chapel period of a small Bible school. As he looked down to open his Bible after announcing his Scripture text while simultaneously requesting everyone to open their Bible too, he heard no sound of movement from the small audience. When he looked up again he was shocked to realize that no one in the crowd brought a Bible. Here is a group of future pastors and lady workers, with no Bible in hand, and who love to preach or teach more of their experience than the Word of Truth.

Church Leaders Are Grounded on God's Word

The Leader Must Identify False Teachers

In 1 Tim 4:1,2 Paul warned Timothy, "Now the Spirit speaketh expressly, that in the latter times some shall depart from the faith, giving heed to seducing spirits, and doctrines of devils; Speaking lies in hypocrisy; having their conscience seared with a hot iron." False teachers will penetrate the church and some genuine believers will be swayed away. How can deceivers enter the church and lead many astray? Here are two methods that the enemy uses:

1. From inside the church

    The Apostle Peter had a great deal to say about this: "But there were false prophets also among the people, even as there shall be false teachers among you, who privily shall bring in damnable heresies, even denying the Lord that bought them, and bring upon themselves swift destruction. And many shall follow their pernicious (destructive) ways; by reason of whom the way of truth shall be evil spoken of." (2 Pet 2:1,2). False prophets arose from Israel itself, and some of their teachings were brought into them as was the case of those who came out of Egypt, or through inter-marriage with pagans, as was the case of King Solomon. In the church, there are some members, particularly some transferees who might have come from churches with doctrinal errors. When they apply in your church they may even promise to subscribe to the doctrinal statement and philosophies of your church. Then, after gaining grounds in your church and even a little amount of influence, they begin to share their heretical views with some individuals. They normally target those they know who are weak in their doctrinal belief, who have problems with their spiritual life, those who are disgusted with the leadership of the church or the worst group of all, those who are seeking position in the church but can't be appointed because the leaders know that they have problems concerning the attitude of their hearts. They will seldom aim for strong leaders in the church but will welcome any immature leaders or minority leaders of the opposition bloc. While some of these false teachers are purely disillusioned, many are laden with evil intention whose chief objective is to take control of the church through a divide and conquer method. Some of these deceivers may not be genuinely converted, and are agents of the enemy whose aim is to bring havoc to the church.

The Anatomy of Church Leaders

2. From outside the church

With the rise of modern day Balaams who use all forms of media such as television, radio, printed, and social media, billions of people can gain easy access to them and Christians everywhere are not exempted. Some Christians ignorantly watch or read their books and have the wrong perception about eloquent and convincing speakers who stand before thousands of people in an elaborately decorated auditorium with good music and message that tickles their ears. They are impressed to hear new teachings and wonder why their pastor at home doesn't teach it, and get a false understanding why their church is not growing and attract more people, unlike the new fraud leader that they witnessed. Some will belittle their home church, leave and join the new cult. Others may get excited, go back to their church and become the new ambassador of a false religion. Sometimes, new teachings become appealing to some believers in the church. Their minds are stimulated into entertaining them until they are convinced with these new "revelation." Pride may be the source of falling into the trap of deception, because they might think that they know something that others in the church don't know thinking that these are only revealed to the spiritually elite. It is impossible that the apostles did not discover these supposedly new "revelations" during their time, because Paul himself told the elders at Ephesus, "For I have not shunned to declare unto you all the counsel of God." (Acts 20:27). If Paul stayed there for more than two years (Acts 19:8–10) then he must have taught them all the doctrines, except a full doctrine of eschatology as the Book of Revelation was not yet available that time. Paul had to teach them everything in preparation for future wolves that will devour the flock. At the last book of the New Testament where the full teachings of the end times were revealed, there was a serious warning not to lessen or add to the prophecy of the book. The New Testament canon has already been closed, so there is no more new revelation or new gospel other than what is taught in the sixty-six books of the Bible. I have a long-time principle for this: "If it is new, then it is not true. If it is true, then it is not new." There are no more extra Biblical revelations, no more modern prophets or new message from the Holy Spirit. And there are no new teachings or interpretation of the Scriptures that appears to be controversial today that have not been discovered by the apostles or early church fathers. Perhaps the reason that they did not mention these matters in their early writings is that they find it too insignificant. Please don't think that God gave you special illumination to discover new teachings from the Bible. Progressive revelation only applies from Genesis 1:1 to Revelation 22:21 where God slowly revealed Himself to humanity all throughout the history of the world.

The Leaders Must Protect the Church from False Teachings

False teachers who enter in or who are in your assembly should be seriously dealt with. Those who are not members of the church should be asked to leave immediately, and the congregation be warned about them. They must be exposed, as well as their false doctrines. If they are members of your church, they must be dealt with according to the guidelines set by our Lord Jesus Christ regarding church discipline in Matt 18:15-20. How they should be approached may slightly vary from church to church but the desired result is to win them back in truth in the Lord Jesus Christ.

How can you avoid false teachings in the church? Here are some helpful suggestions:

1. The church should have a well-defined Statement of Faith.

    A too generalized doctrinal statement may leave a loophole for future contention. For example, we don't just state "We believe that there is One True God, eternally existent in Three Persons." The word "distinct" must be inserted in the phrase "eternally existent in Three 'distinct' Persons" because there is a widespread teaching going around saying that the Three Person of the Trinity is embodied all in Jesus Christ alone. If this heresy enters your church, then the false teacher might use your own Statement of Faith. One word can make a difference. Try reviewing your church's doctrinal statement, bearing in mind the false teachings prevalent in your area, and make amendments if necessary.

2. You should be able to define what is essential (major doctrines), and non-essential (minor doctrines).

    All doctrines in the Bible are essential, but for the sake of defining terms, the word "non-essential" is used here. Essential doctrines are the clear teachings of the Scripture that will affect your salvation and sanctification. Your whole church must agree on all essential or major doctrines. These are non-negotiable. These are normally written on your Statement of Faith. On the other hand, the non-essentials are the minor ones that have nothing to do with your salvation. To name a few:

- the practice of open or closed communion
- dress code
- name of a local church (some churches drop the name of the denomination that they belong to, or use "Fellowship" instead of "Church" on their church sign) as others insist that the name of the church could be found in the Bible
- the belief that the whole universe will be burned and destroyed vs. the belief that it will be renovated
- the meaning of "thorn in the flesh" of Apostle Paul in 2 Cor 12:7
- etc.

These are called non-essentials because they don't affect your place in heaven. Whether you believe in these things or not you will still go to heaven, for as long as you're genuinely converted in the faith. These, however, affect your way of living. You must choose to "agree to disagree" on these teachings and not let these disrupt the unity of the church.

On one Sunday morning, the Senior Pastor of a local church was about to preach on giving. Before he was called to the pulpit, he asked his Associate Pastor who was sitting beside him, "Pastor, do you still believe in New Testament tithing?" The other pastor replied, "No, not anymore." Then the older pastor said, "So do I." But the problem is that the church that both called them believed and has been practicing tithing for fourteen years. The pastor knew that preaching about his belief on tithing will surely cause disillusionment among its members instead of encouragement. So that morning, the pastor presented to the congregation the two views on tithing but he did not challenge anybody to choose which side to believe. He also did not mention what he and his Associate's believe regarding the issue at hand. These two pastors never preached or taught their view about tithing in that church even until they both resigned and moved on to another ministry. While some pastors may not agree on the actions of the two men, let us remember that tithing does not affect salvation, only the manner

Church Leaders Are Grounded on God's Word

of how one gives. Besides, the unity of the church is more important than insisting personal belief on minor doctrines.

3. Your church should have a stand even on non-essential doctrines because some minor doctrines can cause disorderliness or worse, division in the Body of Christ. Take into consideration that some Christians consider some minor doctrines as major ones. Formulating a stand can be done by having a Bible study with all the leaders of the church, coupled with an open discussion. On a healthy situation, the leaders will agree with the views of the Head or Senior Pastor provided that everyone finds him reasonable. Even when the Associate or Assistant Pastor or any leader has a different view point, he/she must submit to the majority or to the Senior Pastor, and never teach contrary to what has been agreed upon. An example of this non-essential doctrine is the cessation of some spiritual gifts like the gifts of miracles, speaking and interpreting tongues. Some believe that these gifts have already ceased, others believe in partial or selective cessation, while others believe that these gifts still continue up to this day. Some churches have this as part of their major doctrine. Some other doctrines that might cause potential division in the church is the doctrine of total inability or depravity of all human beings against the partial depravity view, or the teachings of unconditional election vs. conditional election, or no election, or the pre-tribulation, mid-tribulation or post-tribulation rapture of the Saints. Note also that different local churches have different issues. Leaders must be sensitive so that they would be able to study and discuss these minor issues before arguments erupt within the church. One church even went to the extent of choosing the King James Version of the Bible as the official version in their church. Although they are not a King James-only church, which means that they could use any good translation of the Bible, they nevertheless chose an "official" version to prevent any future arguments by succeeding generations. So it is necessary that your church has a clear stand to prevent chaos in your church once confusions from these teachings seep into the congregation. And if needed, you may include in your Doctrinal Statement some minor doctrines that the church has agreed upon to avoid future arguments. On the non-essential teaching, any member has the freedom to choose which view they prefer but it should be within the confines of accepted church theology and they should not teach it to other members of the church.

4. In the event that the leaders are divided on some teachings, then love should prevail by learning to agree to disagree. There should be unity in diversity on paradoxical issues. Learn to respect others' opinion, don't be dogmatic because you might be wrong and the others are right or vice versa. Never argue with anyone especially in public as this may destroy the lives of others. If opportunity calls and it can't be avoided, never teach publicly your own view as though you are right, but be neutral in your presentation and explain that there is no clear teaching on the subject matter. This is in respect to others who have opposing view.

5. Teach the Bible chronologically from creation, to the fall of man, to the flood until you come to the Gospel of Christ, Acts and Revelation. This will give the church members a right concept about God. Christians who don't understand the whole purpose of God will not only have a hard time understanding the Holy Scripture but will also find it difficult to know God's will in their lives. In my opinion, most Christians who have problems in their characters don't have the right concept about God. For example, Christians who always complain probably don't realize that God did not explain to Job at least in his lifetime why he had to undergo those sufferings. Well, that is our God. He will not reveal to us everything but we just need to trust Him. Some impatient Christians who want to know God's will at once don't understand that God reveals Himself progressively.

6. Most sound Bible scholars will agree that an expository verse-by-verse preaching of the whole Bible is the best method of delivering the message of God. It gives us a clear historical, cultural, and social background on the text being preached. It also provides us an understanding of the purpose of the writer and to whom it was written, resulting in a correct interpretation of Biblical passages and right application. Although this means more study time for the preacher (at least sixteen hours of study per message), it's the best way to go. Preaching is hard work because you don't just go out there and invent what you say or practice the "as the Spirit leads" style. You don't prepare your message on Saturday evening and expect God to bless you and the congregation the following day. There was this Pastor who prepares his message on Sunday dawn, and although he can still make a good sermon outline, there is lack of power on actual delivery. The only exceptions are unavoidable circumstances like death or

Church Leaders Are Grounded on God's Word

hospitalization in the family. If that happens, invite someone to preach ahead of time or preach an undelivered sermon that you have already prepared before. That's why it is important for pastors to have reserved sermons in their arsenals.

There was this "celebrity-turned-evangelist" who was invited to speak in a 6:00 evening service in a church. An hour has passed and there was no sight of him, so the Associate Pastor was asked to preach in his place. Then at around 8:00 p.m., after the preaching, everyone was surprised when a big man broke into the front door, walked on the middle isle and with a big, loud voice asked, "Am I late?" I was the usher that night, and I silently sneered to myself, "No, just only 2 hours!" The guest speaker halted and asked if anyone had a Bible. One of those seated handed his Bible to him. It was like going to war without even a side arm with him. After some introduction, he then said, "let us read from the Bible ... (pause)." There was about a half minute of silence as he flipped the pages of the Bible back and forth. Perhaps he was waiting for the Spirit to show him what to read. Then he found one from Luke 4:18, a good messianic prophecy from Isa 61:1. After reading the good passage, he began to preach, and his topic was a mix-up of everything! Here was a man, without a Bible, without a Scripture text and without a message. He had no business in the pulpit! I can say that he still had a "celebrity" mindset and had no regard for the people waiting for him. What can you expect from his message? It was full of stories, and although some were funny, he barely mentioned any Bible verse. To sum up his "performance" that night, I can say that he was purely an entertainer not a preacher.

7. You must be careful with those applying for membership, especially those coming from other churches with doctrines and practices that are different from your church, even though they are not cults. You may opt to just refer them to a nearby church who has the same doctrines or practices. Don't get too excited to add new members to your congregation. Besides, the normal way to grow a church family is by giving birth (evangelism) and not by adoption (transferees). If there is no church nearby, then you have no option but to accept the applicants. The process could be as follows: you must secure a written recommendation from their former pastor. There might be two reasons why a pastor would not give a recommendation letter. First, the applicant/s might not be in good standing in their church or is

under discipline. For this, you need further background checkup. Secondly, the pastor simply doesn't like your kind of church. In this case, you have the right to refuse membership, but you can invite them to attend. If an applicant is qualified to be accepted as a member of your church in spite of him/ her coming from a different church background, then he/she should undergo a doctrinal Bible Study which aims to address his/her different doctrines. Once accepted as a member, don't be in a haste to give leadership or teaching position. Just give minor ministry opportunities. In a certain church, it took seven years for a transferee to be appointed as deacon of the church. His pastor made sure that there were no more traces of his old practice in his former church. Meanwhile in another story, an elderly member left his church because of some disagreement with his pastor and then he transferred to a neighboring church with the same denomination. The new pastor welcomed him with open arms thinking that he was an asset, without even consulting the former pastor. The new pastor appointed the new member as deacon of their congregation in only less than three months from his first appearance at the doorstep of their church building. A couple of months later, the new deacon created a serious problem in the church, prompting the new pastor to talk to the former pastor. He then received a good reprimand from the former pastor, leaving him the problem of how to dispose of the deacon. Some of you, particularly the older and wiser pastors may find this comical, but the lesson is simple: be careful in giving ministry responsibilities to transferees and new members. Remember, we are preventing false teachers to arise.

The Leader Must Not Engage in Dispute

The Apostle Paul taught the young Pastor Timothy how to deal with false teachers, "And the servant of the Lord must not strive; but be gentle unto all *men*, apt to teach, patient," (2 Tim 2:24). Although the word "strive" here means "to engage in hand to hand combat," meaning real fighting in the church, it also means "to war on words or dispute," as the context suggests. It has the same meaning in Greek with the word "strife" in v.23 in reference to "foolish and unlearned questions." He told him not to engage in senseless debate. Debate in itself is good especially in politics where candidates participate in lively discussion about their platform of governance so that voters can wisely choose. Or in academic debates where students can exercise their critical thinking. There's nothing wrong with debate especially if held in a proper forum where there is a moderator and each side can present their arguments and be rebutted with time limit. But what Paul was referring starting in verse 14 was not to quarrel with insignificant matters as it only destroys the hearers. As leaders, you must learn how to differentiate between those who genuinely seek for an answer to their queries from those who just want to show off and try to prove that they are right no matter what.

One day, a pastor was chatting on the internet when he was introduced to a man who had many questions on the Bible. He introduced his religion and said that the Christian Bible has many contradictions. Then he began to lay all his barrage of "contradictory passages" on the pastor like "did Jesus feed 5,000 or 4,000?" or "did Judas hang himself or fall into a cliff?" and many more valid questions. The pastor was able to answer all his questions patiently and satisfactorily but he noticed that the man did not even acknowledge his answer but just moved on to the next question. When the man realized that he cannot "defeat" this pastor he began arguing on senseless things and hurled insulting words at him. That's the time the pastor realized that the other person was not actually seeking for the truth. With a closed mind, he just wanted to disqualify him. So he politely ended the conversation and never talked to him again.

On the other hand, there are those who are really seeking for truth who may sometimes ask seemingly insignificant questions, but after receiving an answer, they will readily accept it as if they just wanted to know the reliability of the Holy Scriptures. Some of them may ask questions that may lead them to trust in our Lord Jesus Christ.

The Leader Must Seek to Maintain Orderliness in the Church

There is a need for the church to have her own Constitution, bylaws and policies to address different issues and situations, and these should be based on God's Word. And whenever there are circumstances that are not covered by these rules, still, the principles in the Bible must be observed. There are also situations wherein church policies are not clear with what the Bible teaches. For instance, what would you do if your neighbors' house burns down one night and they have nowhere to go to spend the night in, so they knock on your church building and request for a refuge at least for the night? But your church policies say that the church building is strictly for church activities only. What would you do if you're the one who answered the door and there's no more time for the board to convene, and most of the leaders are either asleep or can't be reached? Would you follow the admonition in Heb 13:2 about showing hospitality to strangers, (besides they're not even strangers because they are your neighbors), or abide by the church rules? Suppose you're a paid caretaker of the church and most likely you will lose your job. Well, it's better to lose your job with dignity than to disobey the Word of God. But fret not, mature leaders will agree with you and even commend you for your action.

In Acts 6:1–6, there was a record of the church appointing seven deacons due to a pressing need. The qualities of these men and the purpose of the disciples were all based on the Holy Scriptures (vv.3,4). We can also say that perhaps these seven men were instructed of their ministry descriptions, particularly the scope and manner of their responsibilities in much the same way as we have our church policies today. Each deacon in our churches is gifted differently. Some may be evangelists or have the gift of preaching, some have leadership gifts, while some others are purely gifted in serving. It is therefore necessary that they have written ministry descriptions. This is true to all leaders of the church, from the pastor to the heads of each ministry. But these ministry guidelines should not be placed above the Scripture but are just supplements.

It is a sad truth today that some church leaders are disorganized and quarrel over the administration of the Body of Christ. They quote and debate on the interpretation of the same by-laws as though it is the absolute standard, forgetting the basic tenets of the Bible such as love, humility and submission. These heated arguments lead to a greater damage, even causing the resignation of some church leaders and the division and permanent closure of some churches. Some members even take the church properties, claiming that the properties belong to them as they sum up the tithes that they contributed. A pastor once claimed (I just don't know if it was exaggerated) that a deacon chased another deacon with a knife as a result of their argument.

The Leaders Must Always Seek to Grow Mature in Their Faith

One pastor was right in saying that if only the leaders are mature enough and grounded on the Word, internal conflicts will be avoided. Problems will be only confined on external ones and not within the group. If some leaders think that they are mature enough but their character doesn't show it then they should honestly evaluate themselves, or better yet resign from their positions and focus on Christ for their spiritual growth. Pastors must be careful in appointing leaders. Character is more important than gifts or talent. A person with godly character but lacking in talent will be teachable, and will listen to the pastor. On the other hand, a self-made person will always have his/her own way.

Our God is a God of order and He wants orderliness in the conduct of the leaders of the church. We can see it in the Old Testament by the manner of creation, to building the nation of Israel, to the elaborate instruction of tabernacle construction, to the priestly apparel. Everything is in order. Christ prayed for the future church that we will be as one (John 17:21). Not uniformity, but unity in diversity. Not ecumenical, but unity in truth, because the truth is the determining factor for oneness (John 17:17,19). This is also true in the local church, that the Truth is the core of our worship, doctrine and practices. Therefore, each leader must devote time to the reading, meditating and study of the Word of God on a daily basis. Any leader who does not have a daily devotional life has no business in the spiritual ministry of the church.

– 3 –

Church Leaders Are Prayerful

> "For this cause we also, since the day we heard *it*, do not cease to pray for you, and to desire that ye might be filled with the knowledge of his will in all wisdom and spiritual understanding;"
>
> (COL 1:9)

PAUL BEGAN TO PRAY for the Colossian believers after learning of their faith, love and hope (Colossians 1:4,5). Notice his prayer for them is that they "might be filled with the knowledge of his will in all wisdom and spiritual understanding." He did not pray for their needs first, or success in their ambitions, because there are things more important than these like godly character, spiritual growth and maturity. When Christians are asked of their prayer request they usually voice out their specific needs, particularly physical or material ones such as healing, financial needs or solutions to their problems. But more mature believers would put more emphasis on strength to endure than healing, more trust or confidence in God than financial needs, and wisdom or guidance than immediate solutions to problems. I am not saying that we should not pray for specific matters that are physical or material in nature, but we should put more accents on petitions that build godly character. So instead of asking God to make you rich, why not pray that He makes you a hardworking person, and that you learn how to save your hard-earned money, spend only on essential things, and that you will give generously to the ministry and to those who are in need. This is in contrast with prosperity gospel preaching who gives the impression

Church Leaders Are Prayerful

that money can be easily acquired if you just believe in yourself or in God, which is basically the same for them, or if you put your money in their coffer and God will return it a hundredfold. This kind of preaching ignores the fact that God allows poverty to some of His children because He is more glorified when they are poor.

How many Christians pray to become rich? A lot I suppose, but how many Christians pray in thankfulness to God for what they have, and not crave for what they don't have? How many pray for opportunities to help others in spite of their poverty? Sometimes Christians are too engrossed in praying for their own needs, wants and successes that they fail to mention others to God. Some even pray intensely, kneeling down and weeping before God especially when they are in great need or deep trouble. These are good acts and sincere demonstration of prayer, but how many of you actually pray intensely, kneel down and weep in prayer on behalf of others who are sick, in need or in dire situations? Loving others means doing to others as you would have done to yourself. If you begin to have self-pity, thinking that your suffering is worse than anybody and that your needs are actually not met, here's a suggested solution to that problem: search for Christians who are suffering from a chronic or even a mild disease or somebody with serious family problems (this search becomes easier through social media), then begin to pray for them before praying for your personal concerns. As you do this, you will find yourself in a better position as they are. It will make you more compassionate and sensitive to others' needs.

A certain pastor has a line-up of names of different pastors and workers with varying prayer requests that he prays for on a regular basis. At the end of the list is his name with a single prayer request. What is peculiar about his single prayer request is that it is not for himself, but it is for the benefit of all the pastors and workers and how he could help them in a practical way. Growing Christians find delight in supplicating for others rather than for themselves.

Sometimes while praying, your mind might wander and you lose your focus, and might even forget what you are praying for. A certain Christian adapted what he calls a "Five-Second Prayer." Every time his mind would wander off and thought of someone, he would pray for that person and immediately go back to his prayer. Saying something like, "Lord I pray for (name) to protect (or guide or strengthen) him or her right now," will only take five seconds. Also, whenever he dreams about someone, he would pray for that person as soon as he wakes up. Of course, five seconds is the shortest time to pray for someone but he eventually finds himself praying for a longer period of time, and sometimes in his dreams he would recognize two or three or more persons and he would pray for all of them, whether they're believers or unbelievers. But perhaps you may ask why he would go through the trouble of praying for someone who just came across his mind or dreams. His answer was simple, "You'll never know if it is the Lord who is prompting you to pray for someone who may be experiencing temptation, sickness, trouble or pain that exact moment." Besides, he enjoys praying for somebody who is in need.

When somebody shares a prayer request, better pray about it right away even when you are doing something. You don't need to drop your task to sit and pray, because you can pray with your eyes open provided that you're not doing a dangerous work like driving a bulldozer beside a ravine or cleaning a window on the fifty-seventh floor of a building. If that is the case it could wait when you're on safe ground.

A young man once shared a testimony which took place during the early days of his Christian conversion. One day while walking home, his Christian friend asked him to pray for him and he obliged to do it before going to bed that night. The following day, they met again and his friend wore a big smile on his face, was rejoicing, and told him that his prayer was granted. He thanked him so much for praying for him. But then, he suddenly remembered that he forgot to pray for his friend the night before! He was so ashamed before his friend, that he can't find the right words to say. Most of all, he was ashamed before God. He learned a lesson that day, and that is to never procrastinate when it comes to prayer.

Leaders Must Pray for Their Church

The analogy of the church of our Lord is like a body with Christ as the Head. Since only the Head is perfect, the body, which is the church, is subject to illness or disorderliness—just like a human body. It is important to properly nourish the body with the Word of God, to make sure that all parts exercise their spiritual gifts, and to pray for the body to stay spiritually healthy. Prayerful leaders demonstrate total dependence upon God so that for any success in the ministry, they give all the credits to God alone for His glory. The leaders must also keep in mind the goals and objectives of the church and ensure that they are heading in those directions. It is easy to be sidetracked with activities that, no matter how good, do not contribute to

Church Leaders Are Prayerful

the theme of the church. I call it, "Majoring on the minor, and minoring on the major." Some churches would focus their attention on activities that are good but are not necessary, and neglect the most essential undertakings. A pastor summed it up when he told his congregation, "I have 1001 ideas of activities that we can do as a church, but we'll stick to those important ones only like preaching, teaching, prayer meeting, evangelism, home Bible Studies, fellowship, etc., because these are the things that will help you grow spiritually both individually and corporately."

A church in a remote area with around 30 members decided to come up with a musical drama play with their members as the actors. But the unintelligent part of their action is that they decided to rent a theatre in the big city to stage their play and sell tickets. You can just guess the outcome of their project because city people don't buy tickets on unknown talents, and besides, they don't have a marketing arm to promote the play. Not all good things are necessary, so when opportunity comes, be prayerful about it before grabbing it. Some of these opportunities may be too good and may appear to be very rewarding, but if it is not God's will for you to be in that situation, it will be the worst place that you will be into. At first you might not realize it but later on, you'll regret your decision. While this is true in your church, this may also be true in your personal life so you need to pray hard and honestly ask yourself the following questions when opportunities arise:

1. What do the principles of the Bible teach about it? All your actions from hereon should be supported by Biblical principles. Just be careful not to twist the truth of the Word of God to support your personal whims.

2. What is your motive for doing it? Will you give glory to God or will it just make you feel good and eventually make you proud?

3. Do you have the capability to be involved in it? If it is a church project, do you have the resources to do it in terms of finances, manpower and time? Will the eternal investment outweigh the resources spent or will it only yield little eternal significance, or none at all?

4. What do the older, more mature members advice about it? You should not seek advice from your close friends only, because most likely you would only hear from them what you want to hear. Look for people with godly wisdom who would give you counsel objectively.

The Anatomy of Church Leaders

5. Do you have complete peace in your heart or is there any hint of doubt in your mind? Although your emotion can be dictated by your mind, it is also good to have an honest evaluation of yourself.

You must pray for your church to not to be swayed by new and exciting ideas that have nothing to do with the church's purpose. After attending an international Christian event in another country, a worker was asked by a young Christian lady in the church, "What is the latest trend in other countries?" The worker can't give a definite answer at that moment, because the lady was asking the latest trend in Christian worship and music with the purpose of copying them. Every church is unique in its design and role in their community, and we should not copy what other churches have or do. A pastor expressed his sentiment to a group of pastors because another church has a lot of members who are in the medical profession. He said he also wanted to reach out to medical people so that they can also conduct medical mission like the other church. One of the pastors in the group asked him about the location of his church and the composition of their members. He said his church is located at a commercial building and most of the members belong to the business community. Then the other pastor gave him a wise advice, "Why don't you forget about the medical people but instead put up some tables and chairs in your place, offer free coffee, and send invitation to all the tenants of the building from the ground floor to the top where they can hang around during coffee break. As a result, you can meet a lot of new prospective contacts for evangelism." This conversation occurred during the time when making coffee is simply putting some scooped powder in a cup of hot water, adding sugar and cream, and people interact with each other. Unlike today where coffee is given complicated names and you sit alone in a coffee shop alone by yourself with your gadget and free access to a Wi-Fi connection. I just don't know if his suggestion was taken, but the point is you must pray to God about the design of your church and ask Him for the right strategy and usually, you will find your own tactic as cost-effective, enjoyable and stress-free.

Just like any human body, the body of Christ sometimes is ill but you can prevent any illness by being a prayerful leader. Ask the Lord for sensitivity and discernment for any potential problem so that you can address it before it becomes a serious threat to the health of the church. A spiritual leader can sense if there is a problem in the church while a spiritually mature leader can detect a potential problem even before it comes. It is therefore the responsibility of every leader to see to it that the church is spiritually

Church Leaders Are Prayerful

healthy all the time. Although there is no such thing as a "Trouble-Free Church," a healthy church nevertheless knows how to handle and treat its own problems by the grace of God.

Here are some symptoms of an ailing church (not in order of seriousness):

1. People love to sing more than hear the preaching of the Word.

    Some churches would sing for hours and listen to the Word for a few minutes only, then their minds begin to wander. Remember that singing of hymns or worship songs is just a preparation for the preaching of God's Word. Preaching is the main component of any worship service or fellowship. When the people of God gather together, they come to listen to God's message for them. Some people of the church grow weary in listening to the same preacher every Sunday. If this is the case, then the pastor or the leaders should appoint their associate pastor, a lay preacher, or invite a guest speaker at least once a month to break the monotony. But the better option is to have the associate pastor or homegrown lay preachers preach, as compared to inviting guest speakers on a regular basis. This is because some members think that the guest speakers are better preachers than their own pastor, especially if they have hidden grudges against their pastor. If you regularly invite guest preachers, most likely these members will only appear in your church every time a guest speaker is preaching. I call these people "ungrateful members," who have no regard for their faithful pastor who labors hard to feed them with the spiritual food which is the Word of God week after week. If you belong to these "ungrateful ones," I suggest that you pack up and leave the church at once and go somewhere else where your appetite for a dynamic preacher or someone who will tickle your ears with watered-down sermons will be satisfied. Because you are not only a pain in the neck of your spiritual leaders, but you also hinder the growth of the church by being a contaminant to other faithful members. Now if you decide to stay, you better get your acts straight by acknowledging your sins before God and change your attitude before your pastor. Begin looking at the good things that your Pastor is doing instead of looking at his negative side. Perhaps in the past he gave you some advice, or visited you when you or family members were sick, or prayed in tears on your behalf, begging God for your spiritual welfare. These are some of the valuable helps that your pastor may have extended to you which no guest speaker would give.

The Anatomy of Church Leaders

Now I am not against inviting guest preachers especially on special occasions, but homegrown preachers are still the best. Let's illustrate it in simple terms: when your family gathers around for bonding, pep talk or to discuss some serious matters, most likely you want your dad, mom or grandparents to do the talking and not some expert psychologist, psychiatrist or psychotherapist. No matter how expert they are in their field, they weren't there when your family shared the joy of having a new baby in the family, and during birthdays, weddings, graduations, reunions or milestones. They weren't there when your family was experiencing pain or grief over the loss of a loved one, or of a pet dog, and on times when all of you were stricken with anxiety when one of the little ones momentarily got lost in the shopping mall, or when someone got sick in the family. In my opinion these experts will talk only by the book and not by experience. Your pastor is like a family member who was always there, sharing in your laughter and tears. Begin appreciating your pastors. Love, accept them and be very supportive to them.

2. Guests don't feel welcome.

If you are a guest in a church you would know if someone greets you insincerely. And you would also notice if only the ushers greeted you. Although this is not an accurate gauge because even a healthy church may sometimes unintentionally neglect a visitor or two, it is nevertheless an indicator of a serious problem if it happens to all who visit. A young Christian lady went to visit a church for the first time. She was greeted by a lady who smiled at her, shook her hand, and asked for her name. The following Sunday, she was greeted by the same lady, shook her hand and asked her name again, thinking that she was a first timer. On the third Sunday of her visit, to her utter disappointment, that same lady approached and greeted her, shook her hand and asked her name for the third time still thinking it was her first time to visit! The lady who kept on greeting her was still in her early twenties, and was not suffering from a short-term memory loss; in fact her mind was very sharp because she was a college professor. To some Christians, greeting visitors has become routine, mechanical, or simply going through the motions. They just shake the visitors' hands and turn their backs on them. When you greet newcomers in the church, give them a firm handshake, a fist bump, or tap on the shoulder, or whatever is acceptable in your culture. Look them in their eyes and ask their names, as well as some basic information such as their place of residence, or the name of their companion that day. In some churches, visitors' names are mentioned and publicly greeted, and if your church does this, try to remember as many names as you can. And before you go out, try meeting some if not all of them and call them by their first names. Say, "Hi Annie, thanks for coming," then try to engage them in a short conversation. There's nothing sweeter to any person's ear than the sound of their first name. Introduce the visitor to a mature member and once they got into real talking you can move on to the next visitor, repeating the same process. If everyone in the church will do these, visitors will leave with a warm feeling. Most likely, they will come back again the following Sunday. And when they do come back, be sure that the same people who met them the previous Sunday must greet them again and be introduced to more people in the church to widen their acquaintances. If you happen to forget their first name, which is likely to happen, don't panic, just introduce them to someone in the church and say, "Why don't you two introduce yourselves with one another?" Then politely excuse yourself.

One of the reasons why guests feel unwelcome in the church is caused by the next symptom.

3. Too much fellowship among the members

This sickness is sometimes called by others as "*koinonit*is," from the Greek word "*Koinownia*," which means fellowship. It is the swelling or inflammation of fellowship within a church. Yes, we need fellowship for encouragement, but if we talk to the same people week after week, then we fail to reach out to others, especially to those who are in pain. There will be cliques among the members and no newcomers will be added in the church. Newcomers in your church will eventually leave because they feel that they don't fit in.

One Christian worker in a church noticed one brother sitting alone at the back. He approached him, sat beside him, and asked, "How are you doing, brother?" The man paused for a moment, bowed down his head and began to cry. Little did the worker know how much pain that man was undergoing at that time. He lost his house, his car and his business and was at the point of bankruptcy. The worker just listened, did not give any words of comfort, no Scripture verses given. He just prayed with his brother and promised to pray for him always.

There are times that the best way to comfort or counsel others is by keeping your mouth shut and by listening attentively, unless you're asked for something to say. The problem with us is that when the other person is speaking, we simultaneously think of a Bible verse or counter words to say. That is not listening attentively. If you are asked, then that's the time to think, pause for a while and answer. It's okay to have a moment of silence while thinking because then, the person that you're talking to will perceive that you are listening sincerely. Believe it or not, it's the best comfort that you can give to a person in pain knowing that you are there just to listen. You must know how to listen sincerely and not say anything even though you may actually know many Bible verses. Listening is important especially if the one who is speaking is more mature in the faith or is experiencing deeper pain than you. Take the case of an unbelieving father whose young son died. During the wake, they were visited by a group of Christians and the leader of the group sat beside the grieving father and gave him a barrage of speeches and Scripture verses, aiming to comfort the grief-stricken father. The leader used words such as, "Let not your heart be troubled . . . all things work together for good . . . God has a purpose for everything . . ." Irritated, the father cut him off and asked him, "Have you lost a son?" He replied "No, Sir." Then the father angrily told him, "How dare you lecture me about this, when you yourself don't know how it feels to lose a son!" Then he asked the worker and his whole entourage to leave the wake. While it is true that the Word of God is powerful and your motives may be right, the Scriptures taken out of context and out of line will produce an embarrassing result. Most of the time, a prayer for the family is more appreciated than words. Your quiet presence as you grieve with them brings more comfort than can imagine.

4. Give little importance to missions

If your budget for your choir or food for your multiple fellowships is way much bigger than the budget for missions, then there is a real serious problem in your church. The Great Commission is not about singing or eating. It's preaching and making disciples. If your church leaders are generous enough to release a budget for church outings or fellowships but are too stingy in giving support to Christian workers, or to travelling expenses to a mission trip, then priorities must be fixed. As a church, our chief purpose is to glorify God and our main mission is to disciple all that God has given to our fold.

Church Leaders Are Prayerful

Therefore, we must channel our resources to evangelism, discipleship and supporting all our Christian workers. This doesn't mean that we spend all our church money to missions, but we must allot certain portions of our church budget to worker's support, fixed expenses, building repair and maintenance, purchase of essential facilities, important events, Sunday School and Bible Study materials and other important things of the church. We must do away with non-essentials in order to save more money for missions. You can continue with your outings or fellowship by allowing each member to contribute for the food, transportation or payment for the venue. Please don't use the church's money for occasions such as these unless budget for mission has been properly allotted first, and necessary expenses have been paid for. These activities can be funded by church's money only if there's a surplus. Aside from the mentioned activities, a scheduled trip to outreaches or mission field may be a good idea because this would not only allow church members to have a first-hand experience in the mission field, but it would encourage the workers and missionaries as well. If you have not experienced to be a field worker, you'll never know the excitement, joy and encouragement entailed by the visits of the members of your home church. And the farther and longer you are from your home church, the greater the thrill you will get when familiar faces come and visit you.

5. Numerical growth is by biological addition and not by spiritual multiplication

    The church is very mobile. This means that some church members come and go due to various factors such as work, school, immigration, and others. Therefore, it is important to have new faces added to the church through aggressive evangelism and discipleship. You must teach your people to have deep passion for God and real compassion for the lost. This is not an overnight task as it may take time to develop your church to become a mission-minded body. Sometimes, it may take years before your church may realize their need for God and the need to reach out to the lost. That's why it is important for church planters to instill in the hearts and minds of a new church the value of loving God above all, and of loving their neighbors as well. This must be sustained as the church grows older.

    The complacent members of older churches will be harder to motivate to doing aggressive evangelism and discipleship. Therefore

The Anatomy of Church Leaders

you must create a new generation of evangelism and follow-up team. Include all the church members in training them. At first, the pastor or few leaders will do the work of soul-winning and follow-up. But when new converts are challenged to multiply themselves you'll have an army engaging in discipleship after a few years. Eventually the old members may catch fire and you might even discover that one or more of them have actually had the gift of evangelism. But do not leave out those who don't like to evangelize as it will create division in the church, rather, give them assignment as welcome committee to new converts or visitors. They may also open their homes for fellowship or be involved as prayer warriors for the new converts. Make the old members a part of your one big team. Some of the members may be assigned to food preparation and decorating the church building. You can also mobilize all those who have vehicles to be a part of a visiting team, and the church can give assistance to some by providing gasoline expenses. When all the church members are busy with a common goal, and the church is growing both spiritually and numerically, then some typical internal conflicts could be avoided like gossiping, criticism and arguments. Although there might still be frictions between and amongst the members, you must always remind the church that you all belong to the same team whose purpose is to glorify God; that you all have one mission, and that is to disciple as many as you can; and one common enemy.

6. Leaders or members become too legalistic.

When Christians have the tendency to over spiritualize everything, from clothing, to home furniture, to church activities and principles that are not taught in the Bible, they have problems in their Christian maturity and are lacking in Scriptural knowledge. Some think that all secular songs are inspired by the devil, or attending parties (birthday, wedding, etc.) in the company of unbelievers is a sin, or that there should be a dress code or proper hairstyle. Some principles in the Bible are twisted according to their preferences and not according to right interpretation. It is sad to think that these Pharisee ideologies are mostly authored by people who are long-time members of the church. They have developed sets of do's and don'ts that are not supported by the Bible. Instead of the Bible, they love to propagate these sets of rules to new believers, new church members or the younger generation, and they are very dogmatic about it. Some give meanings to everything. For instance, there's a children's song where a lyric is repeated six times, and then repeated thrice. This is interpreted as the mark of the beast, 666. Well, you can give meaning to all children's song and forbid it to be sang like "Baa baa black sheep," and say that since it's black it represents Lucifer the fallen angel, but isn't it ridiculous? Also, there are some people in the church who seem to find it enjoyable to discipline erring members. Another example is the prohibition of some churches for their members to attend birthday parties or any gathering with unbelievers, as well as certain church weddings. Note that there is no command for Christians to become very selective in attending wedding ceremonies. What the leaders can do is strengthen the conviction of their people so that they would be equipped to decide on matters that aren't clear in the Bible.

About some decades ago, a young guy with three other girls were invited to be a part of an entourage in the wedding of one of their female best friends who will be marrying a known unbeliever. The young man who even tried to witness the groom but to no avail, was so uneasy, and so was his three friends. So they invited the bride to a dinner, and after the meal they broke the bad news that they could not attend because of their convictions. They said it with love and much apology as the young bride broke silently in tears. They separated that night with heavy hearts but they had to follow their convictions which they developed after years of studying the Bible and faithfully listening to their pastors' weekly sermons. Some of you may not agree with the four young people but you must learn to respect them because God deals with each of us in different ways. The only solution that I could think of to correct this situation of becoming legalistic is to faithfully preach the Bible verse by verse in an expository manner, draw out correct interpretation and application and pray for all the Pharisees in your church. Select a book from the bible which you think will suit the present spiritual status of the whole church, and just remember that you won't only be preaching to the legalists but everyone in the church. By using a verse by verse method, you will not be charged by the legalistic members as someone who selects specific verses to hit them hard. As a reminder to preachers, don't preach by secretly addressing a person or group of individuals, but be faithful in the Word. Only say what the Bible teaches, and be tactful in the use of words so they won't say that you're singling out certain members, especially if there is a current issue in the church. But do not back down from preaching what the Scriptures demand you to say. A sin is a sin, unholiness is unholiness, and unrighteousness is unrighteousness.

7. There are other symptoms of an ailing church such as poor or weak preaching of the Bible, poor church prayer life, poor testimony among the unbelieving community, worldly lifestyle of members, division or schism in the church especially among leaders, absence of goals and objectives, and a church board who thinks that they are above the pastor, ignoring the fact that the accountability of the church falls on the pastor. These leaders must be reminded of the consequences of taking the leadership authority from their pastor, which include losing their rewards in heaven. But it must also be remembered that there is no problem in the church that is greater than our God, so there is no problem that cannot be solved. And the first step in solving any problem is by prayer.

Leaders Must Pray for Other Leaders in the Church

The church is not an arena where leaders compete with each other. Rather, it's an arena where they work together as one cohesive unit, with one vision and goal of glorifying God. Leaders must support each other, rejoice over the success of others, and be willing to step in when others are unable to fulfill their duties due to illness or deep problems. A healthy church doesn't blame or rejoice when leaders fail. It understands its leaders and lends a helping hand. It does not gossip or slander, but has listening ears. It doesn't put down its leaders, but forms a support system to uplift them. On the other hand, an unhealthy church gloats over the failures of others. The members love to point fingers, abounding with "I told you so," or "just as I have predicted" comments. They are judgmental and would love to see others fall, never to rise again. And when it is their turn to fail, they begin blaming others for not supporting them. They don't want to take responsibility for their own foolishness.

Remember that your fellow leaders are your allies; you belong to the same body. The success of any ministry in the church is not attributed to any leader but to God alone who determines the result of our labors. Success is not gauged by statistics only, but on how faithful you do your assigned task. God will figure out the statistics. Although we don't totally reject results in terms of numbers, a low turnout might just mean adjustment or change in strategy without compromising the truth. This further means more prayer for wisdom for the leaders of that ministry. Leaders must be sensitive to the needs of their fellow workers. Discouraged leaders don't need your sermon, but they need someone who will listen to them, a shoulder to cry on and a spiritual family member who would pray for them. It is recommended that ministry leaders, along with their pastor/s must have a monthly, bi-monthly or quarterly meeting for prayer, fellowship, sharing, and exchanging of ideas, which can promote unity in the local body of Christ. A healthy relationship among leaders promulgates a unified strong ministry among members that will make them want to be involved even in small means. On the other hand, divided leadership in a church will drive away members. An example of this is a faithful leader of a church who was deeply hurt and offended by all the gossips and slander that she heard from the other church leaders, all targeted towards their pastor. That leader resigned from her position and eventually left the church.

Leaders Must Pray for All the Members of Their Respective Ministry

A church leader faithfully and regularly prays for each member by name. A prayerful servant can accomplish much because that servant knows how to trust in the Lord in the fulfillment of the ministry. A pastor once commented, "A pastor who is not praying for his members is not a pastor at all." This may sound brutal because no pastor has been disqualified from the ministry for not praying, simply because nobody sees his private life. And some job or ministry descriptions of some pastors, this element is missing. But if this is true for pastors, this must also be true to all lay leaders.

Some pastors might argue that it's easy to pray for fifty to one hundred members by name, but if you have hundreds or thousands of members, that's almost impossible because you might not even know their names anymore. That's not actually a problem because all you have to do is pray for your core group, your deacons, and committee or ministry head and teach them to pray for all the people under their ministry. Why is it important to pray for each member by name? Because the church is composed of unique individuals who are beloved of God, each with different gifts and talents, different temperaments, different social, cultural backgrounds and different struggles in life, and most likely have different prayer requests.

Each member is important to the body as there is no second-class member, whether rich or poor, old or young, and educated or undereducated. All belong to the same class of people of whom Christ died. Discrimination is an alien practice in the Body of Believers who loves God and each other.

In this time of digital world, people are known through their numbers. People are becoming impersonal. If you happen to observe family reunions nowadays, you can see that only the elderly ones are engaged in conversations while the younger ones are busy in their own world. Some are glued to their cell phones, sending text messages or chatting with their friends from other places. Some are listening to music through their ear phones, while the younger kids watch television. That's why only a few of the younger generations know their family tree, or family customs, values and traditions. Some children haven't even met their grandparents, and the next and following generations are becoming more and more secluded in their own private affairs. This should not happen in the church that's why it is important for leaders to interact with the members in their respective ministries so that they will know what to pray for each of them. This may mean taking time to meet each of them. But remember that what matters more is not the quantity but the quality of time spent with your members. It might just be a casual meeting with a few minutes of meaningful conversation with them, and that already counts. A healthy conversation between two or more people, no matter how long or short it may be, results to learned lessons and strengthened fellowship.

Leaders Must Pray for the Unbelieving Community

Good leaders pray for the unbelievers in their respective communities. The Apostle Paul exemplified this in Rom 10:1 when He said "Brethren, my heart's desire and prayer to God for Israel is, that they might be saved." His most sincere prayer and wish was for the salvation of his own community, all the Israelites, although he knew that this was not possible. They considered him an apostate that's why some of them followed him wherever he went, persecuted him and wanted him dead. He was preaching to them the very message that they hated, and even crossed the line by going to the people they hated the most, the Gentiles, and accepted them as his own brethren. But Paul harbored no resentment against them, but had a heavy heart laden with burden for the lost soul of his own countrymen.

Church Leaders Are Prayerful

Every one of us belongs to one or more communities, not only in our neighborhood, but also in our workplace or school. Some of us are part of a social or sports club. We are surrounded by unbelievers most days of the week. How much time do we spend in a week to pray for them? A young Christian man once went to their rooftop taking with him his high school class picture and started praying for each of his former classmates by name, asking God to have mercy and save them. Several decades later, with the availability of social media, he was able to reconnect with some of his former classmates and he learned that three of them became Christians. That's how prayer works, years may pass but God will not forget your petition. Although he believes that salvation is entirely the work of God, yet he was joyful that he became a part of God's redemptive work.

There was a passage of the words of our Lord Jesus that Matthew recorded in Matt 9:36–38, "But when he saw the multitudes, he was moved with compassion on them, because they fainted, and were scattered abroad, as sheep having no shepherd. Then saith he unto his disciples, "The harvest truly *is* plenteous, but the labourers *are* few; Pray ye therefore the Lord of the harvest, that he will send forth labourers into his harvest." There are three things that we need to pray about ourselves and our community:

1. Pray for compassion for the lost.

    When Christ saw the multitude, He was moved with compassion. He saw emptiness. As you travel every day, you get used to seeing people whether you're in a small town or big city. Sometimes you are pre-occupied with your own affair and faces of people just become part of the crowd. But if you're observant you'll see different kinds of people: some are walking wearing fine suits and corporate dress, some are wearing ordinary clothes, some are elderly, some are young students, you will see mothers with babies, everyone seems to be in a hurry and could easily overlook homeless persons sitting or lying down on the pavement. Some are driving old and new cars, some on motorbike, while some are driving company trucks. Most of the people you see every day are lost and bound for eternity without Christ, while you are enjoying the gift of eternal life. Pray that God will change your heart and have the eyes and heart of Christ so that when we look at the multitude, our hearts will melt with compassion towards the lost souls. Borrowing a statement from a missionary who was reporting about his mission work during a Sunday morning service, he asked the congregation, "When was the last time you cried and prayed for your city?" In most churches if not all, the least popular ministry is the evangelism department. Many will volunteer for the music or Sunday School ministry or other ministries inside the church but only few are willing to exert extra effort or spend extra resources, to be exposed to the heat and cold of the weather while sharing Christ to total strangers. It's time for the church to wake up and realize that the Son of God came down from heaven to seek and save the lost and has entrusted to all of us to preach the gospel to our own generation.

2. Pray for more laborers.

Pray for more Christians who would be willing to sacrifice their time and effort, go out of their way and leave their comfort zones to evangelize, do follow up and disciple the new converts. Don't exclude yourself because you're part of it. Most Christians are just comfortable serving God within the confines of the four walls of their church building because they are untrained, unmotivated, or fearful to go out and reach people with the saving gospel of Christ. Some even think that if you have beautiful building, good programs, good music and good preachers, you can attract the world to come to your church. In some cases it works that way especially if the preaching of the Word is watered down and does not address matters that might hurt the feelings of the guests. But the people who will come to your church will come for the wrong reason, and some of those who will come are members of other smaller churches who may not have all the amenities that you offer. When Christ told His disciples "I will make you fishers of men" (Matt 4:19; Mark 1:17), they perfectly understood the hard task ahead of them because some of them were fishermen by profession. The reason many Christians avoid this type of ministry is that they don't want to labor hard or face the risk of being rejected. Pray for the people of your church that He would raise more men and women who would volunteer into the labor force.

3. Pray for the harvest.

When Christ said in Matt 9:37, "The harvest truly *is* plenteous . . . ," He was referring to those souls who would be saved. Whether you believe in pre-destination or not, the truth is that God knows beforehand who will be saved because He is an all-knowing God, and we're not. That's why you need to pray and plan your evangelism and discipleship efforts in order to maximize your time and resources. You need to pray to God to lead you to people who are ready to hear the

Church Leaders Are Prayerful

gospel. You may be teaching pagans for a year or two but even without seeing fruit of repentance, you are afraid to stop the Bible Study in their group because you'll feel guilty about it. After that long period of time, you must prayerfully seek the will of God whether to continue or stop so that you can channel your time and effort to other souls who may be waiting. Some pastors would agree that after six to twelve months of Bible Study, it could be terminated if there is no sign of growth within the group.

Here are some reasons why:

a. It may be that your group members aren't really saved or will never be saved. Although there's no way of knowing it, you may reconsider ending your time with them if you don't see any interest from the group at all and they don't come to your church in spite of your persistent invitation, or worst, you don't see any changes in their hearts and lives. By deciding to end the Bible study sessions with them, you can invest your time to more receptive souls. But take time to visit them especially on special occasions because you still don't know how the Spirit moves the hearts of people.

b. They may be late bloomers or some are deeply-rooted in a religion that runs in their families for generations, and it needs some time to demolish the bulwark of their religious foundation. If this is the case, then keep coming unless they lose interest and you feel that you're not welcome anymore. A young missionary was teaching three families where the head of that clan was a woman in her early 60's who happens to be one of the religious leaders of that town, and who allowed the Bible Study in their home on the condition that no one from her family would be baptized by the missionary. The young worker faithfully taught them the chronology of the Bible from Creation up to the life of Christ as recorded in the four gospels. The interest of the group continued to grow and they were excited to listen to the new Bible story in the following week. This lasted for more than three years, until interest gradually plummeted down and until about only three family members were left attending. One of those left behind was the woman, the head of the clan who at first prevented her family members from being converted. Then one night, that woman asked a very surprising question: "How can I be saved?" The missionary then explained the gospel and led her to trust in Christ alone for salvation. Unknown to the missionary, God was working in her life for the last three years as she listens every week in the Bible study. Truly, God works in mysterious ways that may be unimaginable to us. For the next three months, he saw the changes in her until she suddenly passed away and the Lord took her home. The missionary thought that had she lived longer, she could have been an effective testimony to their religious community. But he also understood that because of her deep involvement, she might develop enemies and persecutors from her former religious group and her weak and fragile body caused by a long-time illness would not be able to deal with the opposition. The missionary thought that this was perhaps the reason why the Lord called her home to rest eternally, although he wasn't so sure about it. After the woman's passing, the missionary knew that his mission in that clan has also ended.

c. It may be that they are not meant to become a part of your church.

    A pastor had a Bible Study with a man and his family for several months which required around 30 to 40-minute drive to their place. Then for some reasons, he stopped coming to their house. After two years, the pastor and that man met again in a National Missions Conference, and by that time, the man was already an active member of the men's group in another local church nearer to his house. Sometimes a person may grow in faith in another church, and you must not be selfish about it. You must rejoice because another church may take good care of that person.

    A professional athlete got saved and joined a church. Nearby, another church which belongs to the same group had several professional, amateur and varsity players within their membership. A sensible pastor might have urged that lone professional athlete to join the nearby church because they have a healthy program for reaching other athletes in which he can grow more. But other pastors would not agree to that since he is quite a catch and can add glamor to the church. If this is your reasoning, then you're only thinking of your church and not the welfare of the soul of the people in your church. You're only interested in building your kingdom and have no regard for its citizens. You only think of the image of your church and not for the spiritual benefit of the souls under your care.

You must also plan whom to evangelize because there are billions of different people out there. Plan and pray to witness to any influencer within your community. Because if people with wide circle of influence will be

Church Leaders Are Prayerful

converted, then it will be easier for you to gain access to their followers or subordinates. They are your government officials, company president, managers, supervisors, school principals, student leaders, police or military officers, athletes and others. If you don't reach this people first, the cults will. This is not discrimination against certain people, but rather, it's one of the ways of reaching more people in a faster manner. For example, if you plan to reach factory workers, it may take you so much time to reach each one of them with the gospel since they're many in number. You might also find it hard to gather them. Whereas if you witness first to their company president or to any high-ranking officials, then they can easily mobilize all the workers to meet for at least the first 30 minutes every Monday morning for words of encouragement and prayer. You'll have a captive audience that you can easily invite to meet outside for Bible studies. Even if the officers of the company don't respond to the gospel, it will be easier for you to invite the workers once they know that you are an acquaintance or a friend to some people in the higher management. That's the importance of reaching first the influencer because it saves time, effort and resources. Perhaps your greatest problem is how to meet with these leaders since they are busy people, and for this matter, you just need to trust God and pray. If you have a sincere desire to reach a group of people, then God in accordance to his will may set a divine appointment for you. And also, you may not realize it, but people who has the same culture, language background, profession, hobbies and interest as you will most likely listen because they may be able to see themselves in you.

Never underestimate the power of prayer in your ministry. A young pastor once had to attend a funeral of a deceased cousin, and since no one in the crowd is a known Christian, he volunteered to be the official photographer. After the mass in the church, the body was taken to the cemetery and was laid in front of the people. As soon as he began to focus his camera, he noticed that everyone was silent and looking at him. Since there was no other clergy present, everyone was expecting him to lead the service. He froze as soon as he realized it because he had no experience leading a committal service. When a cousin asked him to start the service, he ran back to his car to look for a Bible but could not find anything except for a Reader's Digest magazine. With hands shaking, he attempted to pick it up and thought of pretending that he's reading from a Bible but eventually dismissed the idea. He slowly walked back to where the people were, and as he stood before them and made a brief introduction, his mind suddenly went blank. He can't even remember the first word of Ps 121 which he memorized, and even used its words as lyrics to a song that he composed. So he just asked everyone to bow down their heads and he led them in prayer. After saying the first few sentences in his prayer, he could already hear sobbing from the crowd. He continued praying for the living, asking the Lord to have mercy on their souls. After the prayer, the service was over. The pastor realized that some of those crying were not even close friends of the deceased. His cousin then thanked him for the "wonderful" service he led. He wondered what was wonderful about the service since he stuttered, there was even no preaching of the Word, and no committal ceremony. What he didn't realize that time is that prayer alone made the difference.

We live in a fast-paced world where everyone is used to doing everything in a rush. To spend time in prayer even for a few minutes is now considered as idleness or procrastination. However, this is not so in the sight of God because it is a holy time of communion with Him. Just as there are occasional breaks in a company for board or staff meeting to set the direction of the workers, we also need to take a short break each day, even for a couple of minutes, to meditate upon God and say our sincere prayers. It may be done before coffee or lunch break, or a few minutes before leaving from work at the end of a day.

One last thing, if you are asked to pray in public, whether in a community affair, a company party, school program or any public function, don't overkill it by preaching first before praying. In one company party, a pastor was invited to lead the invocation. The problem was that he first gave a 20-minute sermon before praying. He was insensitive and failed to see the furious company officials talking at the back. They wanted to stop him from talking, because as one of the supervisors said later on, he was taking the time from the busy employees' party. You may use Paul's command to "Preach the word; be instant in season, out of season; reprove, rebuke, exhort with all longsuffering and doctrine" (2 Tim 4:2), and maybe reason out that you have a captive audience, but make sure that you are led by the Holy Spirit before you do so. You may also argue that the apostles preached in every place where an audience was present. But remember that they lived in another time and culture where people had more time to listen and were used to hearing rabbis teach. We now live in another time and culture where every minute is important and everything is programmed.

In another occasion, another pastor was invited to lead the opening prayer in a college graduation. When he was called, he went to the podium,

Church Leaders Are Prayerful

prayed for about three minutes, and went back to his seat. The college president even quoted a part of his prayer in her speech. While the other pastor was banned from coming back to the company, the other one was used by God to minister to the campus where at one time the gospel was preached to over two thousand students and faculty members.

Prayer is so important in the life and ministry of a Christian leader, and sometimes you need to "talk less, and pray more."

– 4 –

Church Leaders are Servants of Christ

> "Simon Peter, a servant and an apostle of Jesus Christ,
> to them that have obtained like precious faith with us through
> the righteousness of God and our Saviour Jesus Christ:"
>
> (2 PET 1:1)

"SIMON PETER, A SERVANT and apostle of Christ." That's both the lowest and the highest calling in the ministry. First, he was just a servant, a slave, but at the same time, he was an apostle, one of the pillars of the church, recognized as the leader of the group, the highest human position in the Body of Christ. How can a servant be a leader at the same time? It's because he recognized that his calling came from Christ, the real Master and Lord. Had not Christ chose him and called him, he would have remained a fisherman, would have died a fisherman and would not have an impact in the world. In the same way, every member of the church, whether pastor, deacon, ministry head or leader, food server or driver, are all equal slaves of our Great Master Jesus Christ. Your position doesn't determine your rank, but only your role in the church.

One pastor complained about how they were treated in their organization. He said there seems to be a special treatment given to the ordained pastors as compared to the non-ordained ones. The organization thinks that the ordained ministers have a special anointing from God and that they are more effective in the ministry. It is important to remember that any success in the ministry is all by the grace of God. Being ordained in the ministry doesn't give you special benefits from heaven, but it only confirms your calling in the pastoral ministry. Also remember that you will not receive any special anointing or treatment from God once you're ordained because God can use whomever He wants, even "ordinary" church members according to His good pleasure.

One time, a youth leader of a church was able to preach the word of God to over 1,000 students, which was more than his pastor's entire life of preaching to unbelievers that time. This is an example of a ministry success which is backed-up by the faithful prayers of a mother, wife, child, or even an unknown church member. These are the unknown heroes of the faith whose names don't appear in the annals of history, yet they play major roles in the furtherance of the gospel ministry.

Servants Are Humble

Any Christian leader who recognizes that everything that he/she is came from the Lord will remain humble before God. When the two disciples, James and John were dreaming of self-importance by sitting beside Christ in His Kingdom, the other ten became furious towards them. These two even used their own mother to gain a headway over the ten, and this made the other disciples indignant because perhaps they themselves were coveting that position (Matt 20:20–24). It was at this point that Christ taught all of them the lesson on how to be great in the sight of God by becoming servants of all. "And whosoever will be chief among you, let him be your servant:" (Matt 20:27). He even gave them a hint on the road to glorification by means of offering Himself first, although at that time the disciples were not able to comprehend truth in the statement of Christ, "Even as the Son of man came not to be ministered unto, but to minister, and to give his life a ransom for many." (Matt 20:28). Later on, when Christ made His public appearance in Jerusalem, He taught His disciples a real life lesson. He did not ride on a thoroughbred, but on a lowly donkey without a band of armed royal guards, chariots or angelic beings in order to introduce Himself as the Son of David, Who comes in the Name of the Lord. He was accompanied only by His lowly disciples who travel on foot (Matt 21:5,9). This was a clear fulfillment of the prophecy of the prophet Zechariah (Zech 9:9). Yet the Pharisees failed to see the truth because how can a lowly servant be the Messiah? They were so blinded that they didn't see the truth of Christ's first coming to this world as a meek and lowly servant who, as a lamb, was slaughtered to give His life as a ransom for many (Matt 20:28b). And when He comes again, He will come as a Conquering King in all His glory. (Matt 24:30).

Any authority or power handed over to the wrong person will be abused. As leaders, you must be very careful in delegating a ministry to anybody as the state of the heart and humble attitude are of utmost importance. On the other hand, some well-meaning Christians started with a right heart but as they go up in the ministry ladder, they become well-known, money starts coming in, and soon, their hearts become corrupted. Some end up in money laundering, some fall from pride, and some from sexual immorality.

Power sometimes corrupts a Christian if not handled properly, or if that Christian was not discipled or mentored appropriately. Some Christian leaders begin to think of their ministry as theirs or purely as a profession. They begin to compete with other leaders in the church or with other churches simply because they are afraid to lose their job or position. These leaders try to outsmart others instead of being a complementary co-laborer in the ministry. They put more emphasis on the academics than on the heart, thinking more of their job description than reaching out to the needy souls. They forget their calling (if they are truly called) and begin to think of themselves as "professional workers." No wonder the church treats them as employees and not as church leaders. They begin to please people and not God, and avoid hurting people in their preaching or teaching, and then turn a blind eye on immoral acts of rich and influential members for fear of losing a huge financial contribution to "their" ministry. This way, they satisfy the appetite of some seemingly important people and famish those who are truly spiritually hungry. Thus they lose the favor of God, as they continue to measure their success through their performance and not according to their faithfulness. For any victory they achieve they take the credit, and any failure they make is blamed on others or on the system. On top of this, they become very, very proud of their accomplishments and forget the admonition of James in chapter 4 and verse 6, "But he giveth more grace. Wherefore he saith, God resisteth the proud, but giveth grace unto the humble." Without the grace of God, they can't do anything that God would count as worthy. They forget about God's grace and instead focus on their self-effort. As Chuck Swindoll once commented in his radio program *Insight for Living*, "the difference between the church of the New Testament and the church of today is that before they live by experience whereas now

Church Leaders are Servants of Christ

the church live by performance."[1] It seems true that a church can still operate today without the aid of the Holy Spirit as there are multitudes of books today or articles in the internet dealing on the subject of "how to's." Books or articles like "How to Pray," "How to Read the Bible," "How to Lead in Worship," "How to Manage the Church," or "How to Preach and Teach." While some of these books or articles are good and worth reading, the problem with this generation is the tendency to take a short cut, that's why they focus on the "how to's," instead of knowing the doctrine behind their beliefs and practices, or knowing why does the Bible teach on certain matters of the faith. It's possible today that a church may have an elaborate church structure and program, and competent people in their respective positions, but there's no more room for the Holy Spirit to operate, alter or redirect their movement because of their established cultural traditions. They may operate by the number and are in danger of becoming too legalistic and neglectful of the very essence of becoming servants.

Most well-seasoned pastors had humble beginnings. They were ordinary people and some were poor when they were young, and are used to hard labor. Some started out by cleaning the church building or by doing "menial" ministry (Although there is no such thing as lowly ministry because God doesn't measure you according to the kind of ministry you have. The term "menial" here is used to describe a lowly ministry according to how people look at it), like running errands for people in the church. Some came out of deep trials or experiences, while others came out of emotional or physical pain. God allows this to happen to Christian leaders so that they may learn to be humble before God at all times. So when God blesses their ministry, they will bestow all the glory to God alone knowing that they started out with nothing, and accept the fact that all victories came from God alone.

Sadly, some leaders go to the extent of misrepresenting themselves because of the lack of humility. A visiting pastor once introduced himself to a host pastor after the service one Sunday afternoon. Without being asked, he mentioned that he has Master of Divinity degree and that he also graduated with a Doctor of Divinity degree. Perhaps he was trying to impress the other pastor, who was not impressed at all, because he was older, wiser, and more experienced, and no amount of seminary studies could achieve that level. I am not being judgmental towards the visiting pastor, but wait until you hear the rest of the story. Unknown to the younger pastor, the more

---

1. Swindoll, *Insight for Living*.

mature pastor was finishing his Master of Divinity, which is his second Masters-level course in the same seminary that the younger pastor claimed to have graduated from, only on a different campus. And on the day of the seminary's centralized graduation, they met again. The older pastor was surprised to learn that the once visiting young pastor was also a candidate for graduation on his Master of Divinity degree, and they were graduating together at the same time! The older pastor just smiled at him and thought to himself, "What was this man saying that he finished his Master and Doctorate degree?" He was caught flatfooted lying on his face. This story was shared not to condemn the pastor, but to show that pastors or Christian leaders are humans too and can accede to an unwarranted pride likewise. Remember that it is your humble character that defines who you are and not your achievements.

During a value formation seminar of a local police force, a pastor was given the task of introducing the guest speaker who is the National Police Evangelical Chaplain, and he was given a three-page document which lists down the credentials and accomplishments of the said guest speaker. He was momentarily confused on how he's going to read all of it in a few minutes, but somehow he managed to pull it through by reading only the highlights of the gentleman's career. Sometimes, some Christians would love to publicly announce their ministry credentials or their positions in the church especially when they introduce themselves even without being asked. I am not saying that it's wrong to properly identify yourself, but check your motives always especially if there's no need to mention your credentials or position. I admire some pastors, who, when asked how they would like to be introduced would say, "Just tell them that I'm a servant of our Lord Jesus Christ." This should be the attitude of Christian leaders who progresses in their theological studies whether in a formal seminary or personal study. They should be more humble, realizing that they really know nothing about God and see themselves as only sinners saved by the grace of God.

Humble leaders develop more humility as they are given more responsibilities. They always go to God and ask for His grace as they perform their duties. They acknowledge the fact that without God, they can't accomplish anything because it is a spiritual ministry. On the other hand, proud leaders would aspire for more work, and once they have it, they will strive to perform their best through their own efforts. If they succeed, they will rob all the glory from God and if they fail, they will invent all kinds of

Church Leaders are Servants of Christ

excuses so that they will not be blamed for their disasters. Proud leaders are always concerned of their own integrity or their name while humble servants always think of the integrity and honor of God's name. The word "servant" (Greek-*doulos*), also means a "slave," someone who is devoted to another and disregards one's own interest.[2] As servants of Christ, you have been bought with a price, through the precious blood of Christ from the slavery of sin. Therefore, you have no right over your body and life anymore as it now belongs to God, and so, you must use your life for the glory of God (1 Cor 6:19, 20). You are just stewards of your career, profession, wealth and yes, even your own body and life were handed to you to be used for God's glory. You can't claim anything you have as a result of your hard work because everything you have comes from God. Remember that no matter how hard you try, if God will not allow you to prosper, you can't accomplish anything. Knowing that God is sovereign in all things is enough to make anyone humble before Him.

There was a Bible seminary student who has already gone to heaven, and another pastor who was on his way to speak in a camp but didn't arrive in the campsite because the Lord took him home while travelling to his speaking engagement. Some may think that both men died prematurely because they have unfinished business in God's ministry. But God is sovereign and He was never, or will be wrong in His appointed time. We are reminded of our teachers of old who used to say, "Okay, time's up! Finished or not finished, pass your paper!" Knowing that God is sovereign, who alone knows when our time is up, whether young or old, is enough to keep us humble.

Servants Serve the Flock

Peter had an exhortation for pastors in 1 Pet 5:1–3, "The elders which are among you I exhort, who am also an elder, and a witness of the sufferings of Christ, and also a partaker of the glory that shall be revealed: Feed the flock of God which is among you, taking the oversight *thereof*, not by constraint, but willingly; not for filthy lucre, but of a ready mind; Neither as being lords over *God's* heritage, but being ensamples to the flock."

First he said in v.2 that pastors should feed (Greek-*poimein*-to shepherd or pastor)[3] or nourish the members of the church. This can be done

---

2. Thayer, *Thayer's Greek Definitions*.
3. Thayer, *Thayer's Greek Definitions*.

by teaching soundly, praying, counseling and spending time with those especially in need. This also involves careful observation of the spiritual welfare of those entrusted to them, and leading them to green pasture of exhortation through God's Word, prayer and worship.

Then secondly, pastors should oversee (Greek-*episkopeo*-look after, care for)[4] the flock of God. They should see to it that the church is administered properly and all fellowships and worship services are done decently and in order (1 Cor 14:40). There are two ways to oversee the flock:

1. Not by force but willingly, and not by constraint but by motivation (this will be discussed in the fifth chapter).

2. Not out of greed for money but with alacrity

    Pastors should not serve because of money, but with eagerness even with little support. There are respectable pastors who serve even without financial support. Some pastors for hire would accept a call if "the price is right" and some newly-graduate pastors (but not all), would dream of serving in a big and well-established church to secure their financial support. Some don't want to come back to their small churches back home because they have been lured to the city life where most seminaries are located. But the sad reality is that most big churches would only call the best students or those who excel, not to mention the good-looking ones. So if you are an average and not too good-looking student, you may have a small chance of making it big. But thank God that He always looks at the heart, and experience and history will tell us that it is the ordinary people whom God called and used to display His power. Majority of the called disciples were ordinary people, who had no formal schooling, at least in higher education, under well-known rabbis. But they were trained by the Great Master Himself through actual demonstration and explanation. There was neither systematic theology in their curriculum, nor a subject on how to preach, but they preached under the power of the Holy Spirit, such that on Peter's first attempt on preaching, there are were at least 3,000 souls saved that day. Many preachers today are wondering about the difference of preaching today as compared to the preaching in the apostles' time. Some pastors I know would jokingly say, "Peter preached one sermon and 3,000 souls were saved, while we, after preaching three thousand sermons, only one got saved!"

---

4. Thayer, *Thayer's Greek Definitions*.

Church Leaders are Servants of Christ

Of course there was no secret and the obvious difference is that the apostles preached in full dependence on the Holy Spirit's power. They preached in accordance to what they saw and experienced in the Lord. But this does not mean that we should not prepare or study our sermons anymore and just use or rely on our experiences. Remember that their experience is different from ours because they witnessed the Lord Himself. In our time, no one has seen the Lord anymore or talked to Him either in a vision or dream that's why experiences alone are no longer reliable. We now have a complete Bible and in our culture today, there is an emphasis on scholarly and reasoning instruction. Therefore, you need to study the Bible, properly interpret and draw correct application, but when you preach, don't rely on your manuscript material alone but depend on the power of the Holy Spirit and speak as a servant delivering the message of your Master.

When calling a pastor, it is best if the church does not publicly announce to candidates the amount of financial support that they will give unless asked. This should be the last in the items to be discussed with any candidate. There is this story in one church wherein almost all of the candidates accepted the call first before getting to know the financial support that they would be receiving. There was even one pastor, who was married and have four small kids, who committed to help a new church even without financial support. These are true men of God who value their calling, more than anything else.

There are some pastors who are bold enough to ask for raise on their monthly support. Please don't jump into conclusion that these pastors are lovers of money or are serving only for the pay. The pastor's actual needs must be considered, as well as the cash flow of your church's monthly offering, the economy, how much does a regular family need in your geographical location, and the personality of the pastor who asks. If you find the request reasonable, give the raise, but if you find it unreasonable or not viable at least for the moment, a sensible pastor would just accept the decision with no complain at all.

On the other hand, there are pastors who wouldn't demand and just accept what the church gives them because somehow, these men believe that the church leaders will give them an amount that shows how much they are valued. But sad to say, many church leaders don't value their pastors and give them only what's left of the budget. These leaders always assume that their pastor would always understand, and that he knows what sacrifice and suffering means, and that he is a man of faith. Well, faith is good but you can't go to the grocery or supermarket and pay with your faith because they need cash.

A pastor once sat down, took a pen and paper, and divided it into two columns. On the left column, he wrote how much he was actually receiving from the church's monthly support. And on the right, he wrote his monthly expenses. He had to cross out several items that he thought they could live without and came out with only the fixed expenses and basic needs, but still came out short with 70 percent deficit. From that time on, he decided to stop computing and writing down their budget, and started spending their money only on the things needed. But God is faithful and He never lets his jar ran out of oil. Remember that it is God who actually provides for the needs of His servant workers and not the church. But this does not negate your responsibility to support your God-given spiritual leaders and be used by God in providing for the pastors' needs.

For those of you who are first-timers in calling a pastor or those who still have no idea how much financial support is to be given to the pastor, here is a suggested "Support Calculator":

a. Determine the standard of living in your area.

Different areas have different socio-economic cost of living. You don't want your middle or upper class community seeing your pastor walking around in worn-out clothes and shoes. On the other hand, it is absurd for people in a poor community to see your pastor wearing a fine suit, a Rolex watch and driving a BMW. Both pastors will not be able to reach the people in their community.

b. Determine the average income of your members.

Remember to be realistic because your pastor will eat the same food you are eating and wear the same clothes you are wearing, whether in a humid or cold environment. Giving your pastor a support based on your corporate average income will enable him to live a simple yet decent life.

c. Determine the number of people in your church who actually have work or business which enables them to give.

A church may have many members but it is possible that only a handful could give an amount that is larger than most of the members

Church Leaders are Servants of Christ

can give. On the other hand, a church may be few in number but most members are capable of giving.

d. Determine the actual annual income of your church.

Considering the first three calculators above, you can now wisely decide how much you can support your pastor by looking at your actual annual budget. If your budget can accommodate the desired support, then you must give it. But if you're working on a tight budget, then you must re-evaluate your other expenses and do some restructuring if needed in order to provide your pastor a modest and decent life. One of our leaders in church once said, "It is wiser to invest in people than (on) other things." What he meant is that it is far better to support a pastor than any other activities. This is because without a pastor, you can't have any activity with godly guidance. Remember that your pastor is your ambassador to the world. So how you support and treat your pastor is a reflection of the integrity of your church in your community.

Then in v.3, the third exhortation is by not lording over (Greek-*katakurieuow*-control, subjugate, exercise dominion over)[5] the church of God. Spiritual leaders are not dictators who can have control over the lives of others. But they must set an example or pattern of humility, patience, and servanthood. A church leader is not a boss. Some lay leaders compare the church and the company that they are working with. Some don't even know the difference between the organizational chart of a company and a ministry chart of a local church. An organizational chart in your workplace tells who is the boss or the owner and shows the hierarchy or reporting structure. While in a ministry chart, there is always one Master or Lord and that is Jesus Christ at the top. And the senior or head pastor, the assistant or associate pastors, the Board of Deacons or Trustees, the ministry heads or leaders, and the utility personnel are all equal before God. The chart only says the role of each one, and to whom one is immediately accountable to. There are no bosses in the church, not even the pastors, not the chairman of the board, not the Sunday School superintendent, not the youth leader, etc. We must all submit to the Lordship of Christ and to one another (1 Pet 5:5).

---

5. Thayer, *Thayer's Greek Definitions*.

The Anatomy of Church Leaders

Servants Serve Only One Master

Servants of God serve only one Lord and Master, our Lord Jesus Christ (Col 1:18). They only serve to please the Lord who called and empowered them in the ministry. Because of the diverse people in the church, adding the immaturity of some members, not all will be in favor of your position or your decisions. The longer you are in your ministry, the more opposition you get. You might even have secret nemesis who might appear as your loyal supporters but are actually just waiting for your single mistake and they will come out in the open. You cannot please everyone, that's why it is important to please God alone and do all things for His glory (1 Cor 10:31). You must choose either to please God alone and give Him all the glory, or to please people, and compromise God's word as you listen to their voices and end up disillusioned because in the end, you cannot please everyone and you might eventually lose your self-respect. You should rather receive commendation from God than commendation from those around you. With patience, humility, and gentleness, you must answer those who oppose you using the Word of God as the source of your defense. Praise God if they listen and reconcile with you, but if they don't, just commit them to God, pray for them and let God has His own way.

The sad thing is that some of those who oppose you seem nice and supportive but as soon as you turn your back, they begin to criticize you. The sadder thing is that if they can't find any fault in you, they begin to be personal in their attacks. They begin to magnify trivial things like the way you speak, the way you conduct your ministry, and some would even go to the extent of attacking your family. Also, some lukewarm Christians in the church would not listen to their pastor's faithful preaching anymore because of their pre-conceived negative impressions of him. While others are so blessed from the sermons, these antagonists are missing the blessings of growing in God's Words because of their closed minds. They forget that God speaks through whoever stands behind the pulpit and faithfully preaches the Bible, therefore, all must listen, and those who do not are committing a great sin against the Lord.

Servants Serve with Gladness of Heart

Servants serve not out of compulsion, but with gladness and joy in the ministry. This is only possible if you are sure of your calling in your ministry,

Church Leaders are Servants of Christ

which is in line with your spiritual gifts. Have you wondered why ten people, who run back and forth inside a rectangular area with a length of about 91.86 feet and about 49.21 feet wide, chasing one ball, sometimes under the heat of the sun, for about an hour and a half, never complain? It is because they enjoy playing basketball! The ministry is a hard task because you are serving the King of Kings. But for those who are called in the right time and place, it becomes a joyous and very rewarding experience. You must therefore give your best time and effort to function well. In order to enjoy the ministry, you must fix your eyes only on Jesus.

When you begin to focus on the enormous task ahead of you, you will eventually feel inadequate, unappreciated or on the extreme side, you might feel over qualified. Let us look closely on these three downsides:

1. Feeling of inadequacy

    You might feel unworthy, and the work is too much for you to handle. You end up stressed out and you become sick, or get burned out to the point of quitting the ministry. A young lady once told her pastor that she wanted to quit her ministry because she feels that she doesn't deserve to lead. Actually no one is worthy to serve the King of Kings, but through Christ's justification and sanctification, we are made worthy. Also, there are cases of some Christian leaders who say that they are undeserving because of false humility that finds its root in pride. If God calls you in a certain ministry, He will provide you with the right spiritual gift, strength, patience and joy in serving Him. Our adequacy comes from God and not through our own effort.

2. Feeling of being unappreciated

    Some feel that they are overworked, some feel that in spite of the good things they've done, what everybody seems to notice are their smallest mistakes. That's why some end up frustrated, discouraged or in self-pity. A certain pastor, according to one reliable member, got very frustrated at the church and stood at the pulpit one Sunday morning, expressed his frustration and scolded the members for lack of support, and afterwards came down from the pulpit, resigned, and left the church that very same day. Although you might conclude that his actions were wrong and that you can't justify his engagements with the members from whatever angle you look at it, the truth is that many workers feel this way. When a pastor is new in a church, he receives nothing but praises from his congregation because like newlyweds they are still in their honeymoon period that may last up to three years or more. After the honeymoon is over, people begin to notice the imperfections and flaws of the leader, which they might have noticed before but just chose to ignore. Then the one hundred good things that the leader has done for them will simply go down the drain due to one single error in the ministry, whether intentional or unintentional. I don't know why it is hard for members to appreciate their pastors or leaders. I can only assume and attribute it to lack of spirituality and immaturity on the part of members. We must learn to appreciate and acknowledge our spiritual leaders for their love and labor for the Lord. Although we know that rewards will be given in heaven, appreciations are made here on earth. We can blame the pastor for his lack of sensitivity, intolerance or sometimes incompetence but do you know that the members are also to be largely blamed? The questions below are specifically for the church members to ponder on:

How often do you pray for your pastor? For his wife and children? Do you at least think of your pastor's welfare during the day and wonder what his concerns are?

a. If you sense something is wrong with the pastor's ways, whether in his conduct or in the ministry, do you bring it to God in prayer first and go to him personally to confide with him? Or are you quick in telling other members about it under the pretense of "sharing time," or "prayer request?" Bring the matter first to God; seek His will if you need to talk to your pastor. There's no need to broadcast it to anybody.

b. Do you love to gossip, feasting on your pastors and leaders and feel good about it because you think that you are better or holy than them? Do you honestly think that either you or somebody in the church is more qualified to take their positions maybe because of your "superior" intelligence? You should know that if you are not called by God, this automatically disqualifies you even if you think that you are more intelligent than Einstein or have the managing skill of the Secretary of Defense of your country.

c. How do you feel when you gather people at your side to share your views against your leaders? Your next move, if you happen to have enough force, is most probably to oust your leader, replacing him with a person you're grooming.

Church Leaders are Servants of Christ

d. Are you sensitive to the needs of your leaders? Are you aware that your pastor is deeply hurting inside, sometimes with a personal illness or that of his family member? How many pastors have suffered heart attack, and some even went home to heaven, and members were shocked because they weren't aware of the seriousness of his disease? Do you know what pains a pastor? It is when they learn that a co-pastor is experiencing chest pains or pains caused by other disease, or failing health, and they don't tell any church or even family members about it. Well you can say all things against him like being irresponsible, or uncaring for his health and family, but before you jump into any conclusion, try to know his background first. Some pastors who are like that don't have enough money for medical expenses, or don't have a health insurance that will cover all treatment procedures. Others would not like their family to be in debt with hospital bills, while some simply don't want to burden the church or their ministry to be hampered. Pastors are like mothers, who, in spite of tiredness or illness would not complain because they have to take care of their children. They can also be compared to husbands, who, in spite of deep trouble in business or workplace, would keep it from their family so that their wife and children would not worry.

    A young pastor suddenly went home with the Lord because of heart attack and the grieving wife told another friend that she blames the church that he served in. She further said that the church was insensitive and uncaring about how the pastor felt, that he was overstressed and the church didn't even have a hint. On the theological side, we can say that it was God's will for the pastor to leave this world as it is appointed for one to die, but how can you explain that to a woman who has just became a widow and her children suddenly fatherless? Most faithful pastors would sacrifice everything for the sake of the church, and it is a shame for members who can't even offer a five minute prayer for him.

e. Do you listen to your pastor when he preaches or gives exhortation or instruction or do you have pre-conceived ideas that you already know what he is going to say or that his preaching is irrelevant? My advice is for you to repent from your attitude and don't think that you know it all because as I've mentioned earlier, it means that you know nothing at all.

f. On the issue of incompetence, why don't you just send your pastor to seminars, conference or seminary for further studies, with all expenses paid? In a fast-changing world, computers, electronic gadgets, military equipment or even simple household appliances need to be upgraded. Same concept applies to your pastor. Some gadgets like cell phones upgrade so fast that after buying the latest model, you'll find out a newer model in the market. It was once a common saying that some pastors, although they are faithful in the doctrine, are ten years behind in the way they conduct their ministries in reaching today's generation. It was also said that a pastor's five years of learning in the seminary will be exhausted after five years in the ministry. This may be true if the pastor will just rely on his stock knowledge once he becomes too busy in the church with limited time to study. That's why it is important for a local church to sponsor their pastors for further studies. What your pastor will learn is not only for his credentials but also for your gain. Furthermore, please don't burden your pastors with too many responsibilities in the church, and give him enough time and space to study the Word and pray. Do the things that you can according to your spiritual gifts or natural ability. For instance, if you learn of somebody who is sick or needs visitation, just call your pastor and ask permission if you can visit that person if he is not available. You need to ask permission so that no one will think that you are competing with him. If there is a major construction or minor repair in the church, please don't ask the pastor to oversee the labor because he should be in his study. Do you like your food, especially the meat served to you half-cooked, one that is still hard and tough to digest? That's what will happen if your pastor isn't well prepared on his sermon because of tasks that could otherwise be done by people other than him.

3. Feeling of being overqualified

You might feel that you deserve a higher position instead of just doing menial tasks because of your higher educational attainment, wealth, or your importance in your job or community. If you feel this way, then you're missing the whole point of becoming a servant, because it's not all about position or special treatment given to you by the brethren, but it's about your role or Whom you actually serve, and in this case, our Lord and Master Jesus Christ. You are aware how movies

Church Leaders are Servants of Christ

are made. Sometimes you can only see one or two actors in a frame, but there are about hundreds of people who are working behind the scene. From the producers, directors, music composers, camera men, light men, props maker, make-up artist, food server, drivers and others whose job seems unimportant but without them, finishing a production would not be possible. It is ridiculous for someone who works in the mess hall to insist to the director and producer to make him the lead actor instead. He may have the good looks but not the expertise or acting ability. Same thing applies to the make-up artist taking the role of the director. Do not aspire for a higher position in the ministry because the accountability and responsibility before God is greater too. God will not reward you on the basis of your position in the ministry, but on your heart's motive and faithfulness. Your ministry may appear to be insignificant, but great is your reward if you faithfully do it with all your heart.

I admire the decision made by a young female seminary graduate who accepted the call of a small church in a remote place with no promised financial support. Why did she accept the call after spending her time studying in a well-known seminary? Maybe because she sees the need of that church. While other graduates look for a position in large churches in the city, seeking for "greener pastures," or "if the price is right" as they say, this young lady just fixed her eyes on Jesus and trusted His sustaining grace for all her needs. I can imagine the joy on her face when she receives her reward in heaven and hear the words of our Lord, "Well done thou good and faithful servant!"

Remember that leaders of the church are not bosses or dictators who can give orders or bully anyone that they want to, but are mere servants of the Most High God, serving only One Head, One Master, and that is our Lord Jesus Christ.

– 5 –

Church Leaders Are Motivators

"I beseech you therefore, brethren, by the mercies of God,
that ye present your bodies a living sacrifice, holy, acceptable unto God,
which is your reasonable service."

(ROM 12:1).

As far as Greek grammar is concerned, there is only one verb in Rom 12:1, and that is the word "beseech," (from the inflected Greek form-*parakalow*-present indicative active 1st person singular)[1] which literally means, "I keep on entreating, exhorting, admonishing, begging, encouraging you" with the idea of strengthening the believers. Paul, being an apostle could have used the imperative or command form but instead urged them to yield their bodies to God. The infinitive "to present" explains the action to be taken, and it tells us what is being encouraged to do.

Any serious Bible student would easily recognize the reason why the Roman believers were being motivated to offer their bodies to God, with the presence of the conjunction "therefore" that suggests the previous statements made from chapters 1 to 11. There, Paul taught them the gospel, the sinfulness of all mankind, the propitiatory work of Christ, justification, sanctification and glorification of all believers in Christ. And all those doctrines on the present conditions of believers should motivate them to submit themselves completely to God.

1. Thayer, *Thayer's Greek Definitions*.

Church Leaders Are Motivators

A church leader is a motivator who encourages submission not only to God but also to spiritual leaders. You need to teach correct Bible doctrines to your members so that they will have proper application of its teachings. And the best tool that you can use for motivating is the Word of God. Secular motivational speakers construct their principles from a human point of view which is derived from their own or other's experiences, which may not be applicable to everyone. Because there is only one Steve Jobs or Bill Gates, only one Peter Tchaikovsky or Einstein or Michael Jordan, no matter how you follow their discipline, unconventional methods, hard work or rise from crisis and disappointments, you can never be like one of them. You may come close, but you will never emulate their uniqueness as individual. Only the Bible has stood the test of time, and its universal principles apply to everyone. It's the only Book which points us to Jesus Christ as the greatest Model, and if we follow His footsteps, we can achieve His character at least partially in this world, and receive His glory for eternity.

The word "motivation" cannot be found in the English Bible especially in the New Testament because it was derived from the Latin word "*Movere*" which means "to move." "It activates behavior and propels an individual forward toward achieving goals or needs."[2] To define it in a Christian way, it means to encourage someone, creating a need to do what is good. So the nearest Greek word I can find is "*parakaleow*," which was used by Paul in Rom 12:1, which means to encourage people, without using force, to use their sanctified free will to decide to do what is right. You cannot dictate what you want for any member to do, or what you want to be done. You need to motivate and not command; and encourage and not demand. Some may react favorably while others may not, while others may need further explanation on why they should heed to your proposal. You must learn to respect whatever their responses to your motivation are.

Motivation by Exhorting through God's Word

The belief in the source of an absolute truth which is the Word of God makes it easier for a leader to motivate anyone who shares this belief. The best source of encouragement is the Bible, and any godly and spiritual Christian will readily respond to God's word without argument. We use the Bible to preach, teach, convey the truth, admonish, and counsel people so it is the best tool for church leaders in motivating God's people. Although

---

2. Mitchell-Gosa, "Definition and Importance of Motivation."

the Bible does not give specific instructions for all of life's circumstances, it can give us practical principles which we can apply in situations that we're in, given the right interpretation. Some people use the Bible and take it out of context without the intention of obeying, but only to justify their whims and hedonisms. When you use a compass and a map, you don't mislead yourself by believing that it has the wrong direction and your intuition is right. The same thing is true with the Holy Scriptures as you let the Bible interpret itself. In Ps 119:105, David who is popularly ascribed as the writer of Ps 119 stated it truthfully, "Thy word *is* a lamp unto my feet, and a light unto my path." (Ps 119:105). The two phrases have parallel meanings, which mean that the Word of God as a lamp will:

a. Light our way

Travelling in the Old Testament times especially at night time is very much different from travelling today, where we have wider, cemented and well-lighted road. If you're not sure of your destination, you can always use your car's GPS or mobile phone application for direction. Back in the old days, travelling at night may be dangerous even on short distances as you have to take the side road or a foot path in a dark and moonless night using a lamp to illumine your way. Many of the Christian's life's travel is similar to that, where one can only see the next step and the rest of the way is a step of faith. Christians must learn to walk one step of faith at a time so that they'll learn to depend upon the Lord completely. Why doesn't God light our entire path so that we don't need to grope in darkness? Because He wants us to take each step trusting in His grace and not through our own ability. He wants us to use our spiritual discernment, which is saturated with Bible truths, in making choices. That's why it is important for leaders to motivate Christians to use the Word as a lamp to their feet to give them direction.

b. Prevent us from stumbling and falling

Again in the old days, travelling in the dark is hazardous because your foot might slip, hit a stone, a small ditch, or a protruding tree branch which might cause you to fall and break your ankle. Once there was a Christian worker driving home one night after a heavy downpour. He was descending on a winding road on a hill. The road was slippery and wet so he was driving very slowly and carefully on every twist and turn until at last, he came to the last part of the descend which was a long straight road, slightly downhill. With no vehicles on both sides he began to add speed, anxious to get home to his wife. With headlights on high beam he saw from a far distance an object laid across the street and he thought that it was just a vine from some trees washed away by the rain. As he was nearing the object, he slowed down, switched to low beam, and immediately slammed on his brake, because it was not a vine but a 10-foot python slowly crossing the street and it covered almost the entire width of the road! He stopped just in time to let the snake complete its crawl. There was no street sign that says "Snake Xing," or "Python Lane," (although there is no such thing), and he had to rely on his car's headlamp. That's how important the light that the Word of God can give to you to prevent you or others from serious spiritual injury. Just like physical injury, some spiritual injury may heal in a matter of weeks and months but there are spiritual injuries that may last for a long time, if not for a lifetime. It means that God can heal you and forget about your sin, but it has consequences that may limit your ministry here on earth. The more that God blesses you and elevates you to a higher position, the greater your accountability before God, the congregation, and the outside community becomes. How terrible it will be that after ten, twenty, or thirty years of building your life and ministry, you suddenly find yourself plummeting at the bottom because of single disobedience. There are some Christian leaders who fell into sin, experienced the painful discipline of the Lord, genuinely repented, was graciously brought back to the ministry by the Lord, and became more careful, especially on the aspect from where they have fallen. But although God is gracious, don't ever think of going there yourself! The Word of God gives warning on when to slow down, stop, turn around, or continue moving forward. Making your members understand the importance of heeding to God's Word will save them from defeat, undesirable pain and disappointments.

c. To prevent us from going astray

Experienced airplane pilots will tell you to trust your instruments and not your instinct especially when there's zero visibility or when flying through a storm. Sometimes you might get much disoriented and feel that the plane is flying on a level when the instruments say that you're either banking to the left or right. This is also true to ship captains who have to rely on their radar when there are no stars visible in the sky. Also sometimes, drivers get speeding tickets simply because they don't follow what their speed meters tell them. The Word of God is like those instruments, because it tells you what to do or where to go, or warn you not to make a wrong move. When you're still young, there are some mistakes you make that are still tolerable and can be somehow "rectified" because you have plenty of time to go back and reroute your destination. An example of this is changing your major or field of study in college, or switching career. But as you grow older, you forfeit the luxury of time. When you come to the crossroads of your life, you begin to wonder about the path you will choose and where you'll spend the rest of your life. The decision to marry a person or not, to have children or not, to migrate to a new place or to stay, to resign from work and start a business, are some of the issues that one may face. Some may argue that in marriage, "I can always get a divorce, a legal separation or annulment." Although this might be true, this might still sound too controversial especially among Christians. Aside from this, things will never be the same again when you have hurt and ruined the lives of your ex-spouse and children. That's why it is important for all Christian leaders to pray hard and consult the Word of God for every decision that they make so that they can motivate others to do the same. Whether you like it or not, you must be a good role model when it comes to obedience in God's word in order to inspire God's people to follow your lead. A good and godly example is worth a treasure. With the Bible in our hands, nothing could go wrong.

Motivation by Communicating the Goals of Your Church

Some might call it goals, objectives, theme, vision, mission, or mission-vision of the church, but it basically is the direction which a church wants to tread or go to in varied durations of time, and sometimes in measurable or spiritual terms. But for this study, I simply would like to call it "The Goals." Every pastor knows the value of a written goal. There are lots of good opportunities that may come your way, and some may come in attractive packages, but not all good opportunities are necessary in the context of your church. As a fictional example, let's say that your church is relatively young and your goal for the year is to train your members how to evangelize and do follow-up work. Then here comes a celebrity singer-turned-Christian offering his service to you for free for an evangelistic concert. His only condition is for your church to find a big auditorium and rent a sound system in accordance to the specifications that he needs. What would you do about it? You might think of the thousands of people who might be attracted to watch the concert and hear the gospel. It would be a great opportunity for you to advertise your church and your pastor to the community. Isn't it God's will for us to reach more people with the gospel? Besides, an opportunity like this comes once in several decades.

Before you commit, go back first to the established church program for the year, which is to train your people for evangelism and follow-up ministry. Does your church have the trained manpower to do the follow-up work for all those who will respond or at least show interest? Then there is also the financial aspect. You have to look for a large venue which will charge you by the hour of use that includes decorating and rehearsal time. Take into consideration that almost all professional performers need to rehearse in the concert venue to test the sound. Another is the sound system which includes the lightings and musical instruments to be used, plus the sound technicians and musicians which you also need to pay. Remember, the only thing that is free is the talent fee of the artist which excludes the services of back-up singers and dancers if he needs them. You might also need to consider your tri-media promotion that is printed, radio and local television station advertisement, in which air time is so expensive depending on your location and the network you choose. All of these do not yet include the travel and food expenses during the months of preparation and promotion. Normally, a concert of this magnitude requires a church preparation of at least six months to one year. Three months is only possible if you are a concert production company with ready staff and facilities available. Since this is not in your annual church budget, it will be a huge financial burden unless you have large surplus in your church account. But even if you have the money to spare, again the question of alignment with your church goal must be the primary concern. How can you handle the situation if there are about 500 people who responded and expressed interest for a Bible Study if you only have around a hundred members and only twenty people involved in your evangelism and follow-up training? A pastor once said, "Never evangelize anyone within your reach if you have no intention of doing follow-up work." This may sound extreme but he just wanted to emphasize the importance of doing follow-up work.

The Anatomy of Church Leaders

Suppose the concert pushed through and your church rejoiced because of those who professed faith in Christ and have shown interest in the gospel. To tell you frankly, the excitement brought about by the concert will fade in a matter of days, and after several weeks and months, it will be forgotten. The real joy that will last for eternity will come from the number of people from that concert who were actually baptized and became responsible disciples in your church.

The best thing to do in this situation is to channel the project to a bigger, older and more stable church or churches in your community. Your church can also work in partnership with them. Given this arrangement, those who will respond will be divided amongst the participating churches, and you must only follow-up the contacts based on your ability as a church. Another option is simply giving the project to a bigger church and be in partnership through prayer. The ministry is not about who gets the credit or who gets advertised, but it is all about glorifying God, whether you're recognized or not because your reward is waiting in heaven.

There was once a new Christian convert who was on fire and managed to lead a home Bible Study where he faithfully taught week after week. He even paid for his transportation fare using a portion of his meager allowance. However, due to some disappointing reasons, he stopped coming and he didn't know that the Bible Study continued and eventually became a local church. He only learned about it when he was invited to the young church's first anniversary. During the narration of the church's history, he was deeply hurt because his name was not even mentioned as one of those who pioneered the work. It was only after he grew mature and highly-motivated that he realized that appreciation or recognition is not a big deal, and what matters is that you've done your small part in the bigger picture. Again, do not be lured by awesome opportunities, but always take time to pray. Sometimes, people who offer you with some great projects will demand immediate decision. But you need time to pray and consult your people. If they can't wait then let it pass. It only means that it's not for you. Don't be caught up with advertisements that say, "Call now, promo ends today!"

Sometimes, the ministry can be very tiring, discouraging or frustrating to your members especially when the long-term goals of your church are far from being realized. Nowadays, the virtue of waiting seems to be lost in this fast-paced generation where people want immediate results. That's why it is important to communicate your goals to all your church members. This can be done by constantly reminding them of your goals every time

Church Leaders Are Motivators

you have a ministry meeting, or have these printed and posted where everyone can see them easily. Any progress, no matter how small it may seem, must be shared to your people with excitement.

In 1990, an International Missions Conference was held in Seoul, South Korea. During one of its session breaks, a group of several pastors gathered around a missionary who was excitedly sharing and detailing his ministry experience in Afghanistan. He was even challenging some of his audience to come and help them as God is now opening doors. Somebody from the audience asked him how long has he been serving in Afghanistan and he said, "Seventeen years." Another asked, "In your seventeen years of stay, how many were converted in the Christian faith?" And without any trace of disappointment on his face but only pure expectation, he replied, "None yet!" Now, how many of you would like to serve in the same place for seventeen years with no apparent result? Perhaps some of us will pack up and go home after three or five years of fruitless ministry.

But what keeps that missionary going after years of labor? He is a mission-oriented man, like a soldier who is willing to obey his superior and will finish the task no matter what, and will be willing to die if need be. If their commanding officer tells soldiers to hold their line and guard their post, they will do so, even if all communication is lost, ammunition and food are fast-fading, with no outside support in view. These soldiers will never abandon their post unless they are told so by an immediate superior. There will be no retreat and no surrender. This describes that missionary because he understood his mission and his goal. He knew that with just a single soul coming to faith in our Lord Jesus Christ, the whole of heavenly hosts will be rejoicing. Remember that if you are called to serve in a place. No matter how long your work is with no seemingly visible results, what you're doing is not in vain because God may just be using you to prepare the way for the next batch of workers who may harvest what you've planted. The ministry is like building a huge machine where every part is ordered from different manufacturers. Sometimes those who make the nuts and bolts have no idea of what it will be used for, but they just need to comply with the required specifications ordered from them. Once the machine is completed, they will realize or see their contribution. You need to motivate God's people by constantly reminding them of your goals. They need to understand that everything you do in the church is towards the fulfillment of church goals. Your goals are the factors from which you base your choices on what and how you do the ministry. Always remember that not all good things are necessary. Always consider the necessity of what you are doing by going back to your church goals.

Motivation by Personal Dealing

It is a fact that the church is composed of variety of people, not only in personality but also in spiritual maturity and spirituality. Although time and maturity should go together, but not all who are Christians for a longer time are spiritual or spiritually mature. Some are still sensitive, some are only knowledgeable of Bible facts, but never understand the essence of the doctrines. Others are worst—they are too critical, are gossipers or backbiters that their pastors sometimes wonder if they are truly converted. On the other hand, there are some who are spiritual regardless of the length of time that they have been converted.

It is encouraging for a leader to motivate the spiritually mature and spiritual, but disheartening to deal with the immature and unspiritual. Here are some suggestions in dealing with this second group of people:

1. You should first begin by listening to their complaints, criticisms and rants without contradicting them. Some of them just wanted to be heard. Just thank them for airing their concerns, and if you think some of their grievances are valid, just promise them that improvements will be made on the situations.

2. Then ask for their suggestions on how to correct the situation. You don't need to follow their advice because sometimes you may find absurdity in what they say. Politely conclude your conversation by saying, "Thank you for your suggestions. I will bring this up in our next leaders' meeting and see how this can effect change in our ministry." Be true to your word, share the suggestion made to your leaders, and don't laugh about it no matter how weird it may sound, because for the complainant, it was an honest opinion. Learn to respect that, and try to find wisdom, if any, out of it. And please don't make a long argument or debate about it in your leaders' meeting, just take it or leave it. Some of the complainants don't really care if their comments are taken or not because as previously mentioned, some just wanted to be heard, and wanted to feel that they have a part in the decision-making of the church. A new pastor of a church made a wise move when the first meeting he called in the church was with the elderly members who

Church Leaders Are Motivators

were the pioneers. He let almost everyone voice-out their evaluations and recommendations for the improvements of the church. What is significant in his move was that the elders felt that they were given importance, that they made their contribution, and did not feel that they were left out. As a result, he was able to minimize future frictions with the elderly and pioneers. Again, just listen and don't argue, because you're trying to open a line of communication. Be patient.

3. After they're done talking, shift gear by asking personal questions like, "How's the family, your wife, children or parents?" Be sensitive in the way you ask your questions, some of them might be having a deep marital or family problem and their complaining expressions may just be a cover up of their true status.

4. Take time to know them better. For every problem there is a root cause. Sometimes their untoward behavior is only superficial because there is a deeper problem within. Dealing with a person, as Larry Crabb once suggested, is like peeling an onion by removing it layer by layer until the core is revealed. The outer layers are just symptoms of the source or core of the problem. Sometimes their hatred, anxieties or critical spirit are just the outer layers of their true selves because what lies beneath is the true source of their problematic behavior which can be traced back to their childhood experiences. As you remove each layer, you go deeper in the person's inner sanctum. It might be a childhood trauma, abusive parents, sexual molestation, death of somebody very close to them, broken family, guilt or a very painful experience in the past that caused them to be bitter in life as these past experiences may define who they are now. Even though Christians have been forgiven of all their past sins and become a new creation in Christ, some believers are still haunted by guilt and still cling to the painful past because of the harm done to them. And sometimes, they may be oblivious about it. Therefore, you have the responsibility not to only know them but also to help them come out of their shells. You can start by praying for them and by asking the Holy Spirit to guide you in your conversation. Begin by asking them simple questions like the usual "How are you today?" Ask about their families or work, and try to look for something in their answer that can lead into a more personal matter. For example, when a person says, "Well, work is fine but I got angry at one of my co-worker yesterday because . . . ," then you can say, "Well that's sad to hear. By the way how angry were

you? Were you extremely angry or like angry, angry?" You can add a little humor so that the person may feel relaxed but not to the point of making him/her feel that he/she is being laughed at or condemned by you. Whatever the answer is, focus on the issue of anger and make a follow-up question. Always be polite in asking question and don't make the other person feel that he/she is undergoing investigation or counseling with you as you go deeper and personal with your questions. You can continue by saying, "I know this may sound personal, but may I know, in normal circumstances, what triggers your anger towards others?" Listen carefully, don't judge or condemn, try not to comment as your goal is to get into the core of their problem. Don't overkill, don't be fast in opening your Bible and counter with a Bible verse every answer that you think is wrong. Or else, the person you're talking to will shut down and never reboot or talk to you again. Just like when you're peeling an onion, do it layer by layer until you get to the core. Try to have the person build confidence in you because exposing a person's inner self may be embarrassing for him or her, and unless the other person feels that you can be trusted, you won't have success in your endeavor. So be sensitive and don't force any answer. Once you get to the core of the person or the root problem, try to be understanding because by now, you get to know the person. You may also notice a change of your attitude towards that person. If before, what you felt was resentment, now you'll have sympathy. If there was bitterness in your heart, now there will be pity because you have come to realize that your brother/sister in the Lord needs help. On some occasions, some will even cry, and in these situations, just let them be and don't say a word. Remember Rom 12:15b? To "... weep with them that weep." You may not be literally crying with the person, but offer your sympathy, because you'll never know how much pain that person feels when an old wound is exposed. Offer your prayers and read or quote a verse in the Bible to address the issue. Be careful in giving advice, especially if it's unsolicited. Remember that the person may not like you at all before your conversation and your prayer to God is more powerful than any advice that you can give. Give advice only if you're sure that you are led by the Holy Spirit to do so. They may need to acknowledge before God any sin done in the past, but assure them that the blood of Christ has already covered their past sin and that He has already forgiven and forgotten it. Now, it is their turn to forget and

Church Leaders Are Motivators

let go of their guilt, and perhaps, forgive someone who has hurt them in the past. Lastly, please don't tell anyone about what you know, not even to any members of your family whether in the form of a "prayer request," or inquiry, unless you're given the permission to do so. If you're a pastor, never use the person in your sermon illustration, even anonymously, because some observant members may discover who the person is. You'll never know whose hands the information will fall, and the damage it will create to the person you've helped.

5. Note that the past will keep haunting them unless it is properly dealt with, and they will continually be a nuisance to the leaders of the church.

6. If, after all your effort is exhausted and they still don't want to cooperate, just leave the matter to God and don't stop praying for them. Don't give them any leadership position in the church. Just let them attend, and you focus on those who are willing to submit and cooperate. You can give them minor ministries like assisting in the ushering or beautification of the church building. They may or may not accept, depending on how much or how less they dislike you, but don't forget to appreciate their labor because that's what they need. Just keep on doing God's work with the submissive members, and leave them be, unless they are already doing harm to others and to the church. You can deal with them again in the future.

As a leader, you need to motivate and not just give orders as it is hard for anybody to submit and do what is asked without fully understanding why obedience is needed. Properly motivated believers willingly serve the Lord even when everyone else turns their back, or loses interest, or loses the grip on their vision.

Once, in a church prayer meeting, nobody came but a middle-aged man. He did not go home but prayed alone in the chapel. He knew that he had an appointment with God to pray that night, so he did it alone. Greatly-motivated Christians will always look for opportunities to help the cause of the church and will always seek for ways to serve the Lord in whatever way they can. They don't criticize, they are not in the habit of fault-finding, and they are not just passive observers. They actively participate in the affairs of the church. They are always willing and will find ways to make themselves available to be used by the Lord. There are lots of Christian families who migrated abroad in search for a better life, and the first thing they do is to look for a church where they can worship and serve because they are highly-motivated. Other Christians, on the other hand, suddenly get lost in the crowd of worldliness and materialism as soon as they set foot in their new land of opportunity. It is sad to hear of a pastor who left the ministry when he arrived in the United States and after getting a secular job. However, we should not condemn people like him because we don't exactly know what he's going through. All we can do is pray for people like him.

Church leaders are motivators. They have high tolerance for different people's behavior, and have deep threshold for patience. They need to know each of their members in a more personal way so that they would not be judgmental when listening to their members' complaints, or when dealing with their attitude or even with their annoying tantrums. They are not easily hurt when others oppose them or when somebody doesn't do their assigned tasks. They are not concerned if others don't recognize or even appreciate their sacrifices and hard labor because they know that they faithfully do their tasks for God alone and His reward is waiting for them in heaven. With their focus always heavenward, they are always ready to encourage and inspire God's people to do the right thing.

– 6 –

Church Leaders Are Role Models

"For I have given you an example, that ye should do as I have done to you."
(JOHN 13:15).

Christ's Example

JESUS GAVE A PERFECT example of servant leadership when He washed the feet of His disciples. It was supposed to be the work of servants to wash the feet of visitors because of the dirty and dusty roads outside. For Christ, it was a voluntary humiliation aimed to set a pattern for the disciples to imitate. Christ demonstrated not just the mere act, but the attitude of a humble heart that is willing to serve. When Christ asked them to do something, He always showed them by example. He exemplified prayer by demonstrating to them His prayer life in which he finds rest and strength by communicating with the Father. No matter how busy and tiring the previous day was, He would still rise up early in the morning to pray (Mark 1:35); and He would end the day praying alone with the Father (Mark 6:46). He showed compassion for the lost souls to demonstrate one of the pre-requisites of evangelism. He showed sympathy by crying for a dead friend, He showed them what it means to trust God by sleeping through the storm while on a boat, He modeled humility by taking the form of a servant, and obedience by dying on the cross (Phil 2:5–8). Christ did not do these things for the sake of demonstration only, because these were a part of His lifestyle, and were naturally embedded into the very fabric of His character.

The Anatomy of Church Leaders

Biblical Example

Paul urged us not to be conformed to this world. If we are seeking for role models, the Bible is full of them. First and chief of all is that we should have the mind of Christ (Phil 2:5), the obedience of Noah and Abraham, the leadership of Moses, the bravery of Joshua, the resoluteness of Esther, the hard labor of Ruth, the heart of David, the hospitality of Lydia, the boldness of Paul, the encouragement of Barnabas and many more men and women whose faith is recorded in the Holy Scriptures. The world has highly commercialized the prototypical ways of how we should be. With faster means of communication, it has exposed an almost unachievable role modeling for the majority of the populace. It has dictated how every people should live, and that's why people crave for more of almost everything. If you are not rich and famous, you are nothing and most likely have very few friends or none at all. If you are short, fat or thin you are not so good looking. If you show weakness most likely you will not succeed in this jungle-like world, or you'll be just bullied around. If you are not intelligent enough or has no connection at all, you have no right to go to college because competition is very tough in any field so you settle for "low jobs" like garbage collection or monkey grease perhaps. The world's standard is based on your jewelries, what kind of house you're living in, or if you look like that model in a magazine, and character seems secondary. Living modestly, honestly, purely or truthfully have become things of the past, being surpassed by external looks, outward piety and visible character.

If you would ask a typical teenager to describe his ideal girlfriend, most likely he would like a good-looking one—never mind if that person has a bad attitude. Their reason is quite simple: you can change the character, but not the face. But what they don't know is that no one can change any person's character, especially the heart. Women, especially the younger ones, also have this wrong notion that they can change an alcoholic, a gambler or a philandering boyfriend's habit once they've agreed to marry him just because he promised that he will be a better husband. On the other side, people may be morally upright but their hearts remain corrupt. As the Prophet Jeremiah pointed out about the people of Israel, which is also true for all human beings, "The heart *is* deceitful above all *things*, and desperately wicked: who can know it?" (Jer 17:9). This was reiterated by the Apostle Paul in Rom 3:10 "As it is written, There is none righteous, no, not one:" Only God can change the heart of any person. All human beings living in this world whether in the past, present or future are spiritually dead

Church Leaders Are Role Models

in their sins (Eph 2:1,5). They are like physically dead people who are not aware anymore about the world of the living, of those weeping for them, and can no longer appreciate any heart-warming eulogy attributed to them. And so, spiritually dead people have no awareness of the spiritual things of God and can neither appreciate nor understand the truths of the Holy Scripture. They may be able to know some general truths like the existence of a loving God but they will not fully understand that God is holy and just. Or they may believe the historicity of Christ dying on the cross in the first century A.D. but never able to comprehend the personal significance of Calvary in their personal lives.

The Bible is full of names of godly and righteous people who are worthy of emulation. Note also that most of these godly people's sins and mistakes were recorded, so they may serve as a warning for us. From the sin of Adam and Eve, the patriarchs of Israel, to Samson, down to King David and Solomon, to the denial of Peter, and the sharp arguments of Paul and Barnabas, all were written for us to know that once we put God out of the equation, we surely will falter. But let us focus on how the Lord used their lives and made them obedient to His will. Some may say that David and Solomon are not worthy to become kings of God's chosen nation because of their adulterous lives, and the same is true with Samson and Abraham who fell because of the women in their lives. Some might even say that Peter should have been disqualified as a disciple because He denied the Lord, not just once but thrice. Or that Paul and Barnabas should have been banned or at least temporarily suspended from doing missionary work on account of their publicly-known sharp dispute over John Mark. People who may think this way don't understand how the grace of God operates in the lives of imperfect people. God's grace works in the faulty lives of people who are humble before Him (1 Pet 5:5b). Note also that humility comes from God's grace too because it is absent in our nature. God chooses His leaders according to His sovereign will and not based on personal merits. As in the case of Paul and Barnabas, the Bible is silent whether the church leaders took any action against the two or how extensive the damage that they may have inflicted on the church or on new believers, if there were any. Where the Bible is silent, let us not make any conclusion, but rather focus on how, through God's grace, these men were mightily used in the mission field in spite of what has transpired between them. Remember that God can use you in spite of your mistakes in the past. Ask Him to make you repentant, to be humble always, and to have a servant attitude.

The Anatomy of Church Leaders

Secular Example

A servant leader is a model and does first what he/she asks others to do. We live in a time where role leadership is easily accessible either through tri-media or social media. What I mean is that the lives of past and present celebrities, political or religious personalities are easily communicated around the globe, and people everywhere imitate the people they idolize. So whether it's their ideologies, philosophies, lifestyle, fashion or any commercial brands they wear or use, their followers emulate them because they believe in them. These popular personalities, whether they exemplify good or bad role modelling, could still find bands of followers from among their adoring fans. Unfortunately, even some Christians unconsciously adapt their values and lifestyle in accordance to what the world dictates. I am not saying that all secular people cannot be our role model. We can admire their heroic deeds, acts of charity and some good principles they hold on to, but not their person. Even Christians, especially the young people become obsessed with celebrities and unknowingly set their life's pattern to worldly standards. Some even adapt the language of the world as revealed in the way they communicate through social media. You can see some Christians using unkind or indecent words out of amusement. They may think it's funny or they may blurt those words out due to anger, and because of this, we can't distinguish a believer from an unbeliever anymore. Secular music may have also infiltrated the lives of church members. They love to sing popular songs without examining the lyrics first, although we should not discount the fact that there are some secular songs that are good and are not provocative or sexually-oriented. This may also be true with popular Christian songs that are being sung without checking the lyrics or the integrity of the singer, composer or producer. That's why it is important for Christian leaders to set a good example in speech, in character and in life choices to put to shame those who are living in worldliness.

A young Christian man was left by his Christian girlfriend for an unbeliever because the other guy was well-groomed and a good dresser. After a few years, the brokenhearted young man became a doctor and an officer in the army, while his naive ex-girlfriend was with a well-groomed sales agent whose wallet is empty and is always stressed out due to sales quota. Sometimes we base our choices on our five physical senses, leaving out our spiritual senses. We tend to forget our spiritual values once we meet someone who is outstanding based on worldly standards. We should not be carried away or bedazzled by people with beautiful pearly-white teeth

Church Leaders Are Role Models

smile, wearing false lashes, with those pointed nose and nice cheekbone highlighted by makeup, wearing expensive clothes and driving expensive cars. Strip away all of these things from these people and let them wear ordinary clothes, and you can see the real person inside them. It's sad to say that there are some intelligent Christian ladies falling into prey by sweet-talking men. They easily forget the hundreds if not thousands of preaching and teaching of God's Word that they've heard in church or Bible studies once they hear the flattery of these lying men. Some were left crying, regretting how foolish and naive they were, falling into the evil scheme of these vicious men. So my advice to all Christian ladies is to never entertain or even go out on a date with unbelievers who are trying to win your heart no matter how kind, thoughtful or handsome they may be. If they are believers, be sure that they are growing spiritual Christians who love the Lord more than they love you. It's better to live alone and wait for the right one than to fall into the hands of the wrong person. Even if being a Christian is what you are looking for in a life partner, you might still end up with the wrong Christian if you don't pray and seek God's will. They say that kind and thoughtful words can be rehearsed and that beauty is only skin-deep, that's why you have to look deeper. Look at the heart of a person. Don't be intimidated by someone richer than you, more intelligent or better looking, remember that you are the child of the King of kings, and your citizenship and permanent residence is in heaven, and someday bound for perfect holiness when you reach glory land.

A very pretty teenaged girl whom we met in a church service one Sunday afternoon was in a car accident. Her car was hit by another car driven by a drunken teenage boy. She barely survived that mishap and she lost her speech, her mobility, her bright future ahead, as she is now pinned down on wheelchair for the rest of her life. She depends on her dad to carry her, and her mom does even the simplest thing like combing her hair and brushing her teeth. Her mother confided in us in agony, showing us pictures of her daughter before the accident as a young, active girl smilingly sitting in her red car. She also showed some pictures during the horrible accident, then the pictures of her in the hospital. You may say that the young girl is now hopeless as she lost everything, and someone in her condition might even consider committing suicide if given the chance, but no, she hasn't lost everything because she still has that wonderful part of her life, her heart. That afternoon during the service, her face radiated with joy as she sat there quietly listening to the preaching and singing of hymns. If God looks at

The Anatomy of Church Leaders

the heart and not on the outside appearance, so we must do the same. I am not saying, especially to single Christians, to totally ignore the external appearance or status of the person you want to marry. Surely, you don't want to marry a person with a good heart but has no sense of fashion or proper grooming, jobless, or whose every interest in life is totally different from yours because you will have to spend the rest of your married life not talking to each other because you have nothing to talk about. What I mean is to find a person who is spiritual and mature enough for you, whose one aim in life is to glorify the Lord, and who loves God above all. External appearance comes in second.

We may also hear of immature church members who transfer to another church because they think that the pastor there is a better speaker than their pastor back home, or the music there sounds more professional, or the ambiance is almost perfect. I am not saying that it is wrong to transfer to another church especially if distance is a consideration, or if the schedules of their multiple services fit into your busy schedule, but isn't Christ preached in both churches? It is also wrong to think that the people in the new church are more Spirit-filled than those in the old one, although sometimes it is the case. Now if you happen to hear both the preacher in a small church with around thirty to fifty members, and the preacher in a big church with thousands of members, you would probably notice one thing: both preacher's message content is basically the same, the only difference is that the latter's preaching is more high-sounding as he uses technical, corporate or complicated terms. Then why is the second preacher more appealing to many Christians? It's because many Christians have adopted a worldly standard of listening to seminar or conference motivational speakers, who always use the right word at the precise time, thinking it as heavenly language. This is very much unlike the small-church preacher who uses simple words that are being understood even by simple folks. It is a fact that food with less preservatives, or the organic ones are more healthy and nutritious to eat, so a message spoken in direct and simple words cater to the needs of the soul. Besides, many Christians think that even the Bible, particularly the different English translations use high-sounding and archaic words. But many Christians do not know that the New Testament was not written in Classical Greek being employed by the Greek philosophers or writers surrounding that era, but instead, it was written in *Koine* Greek which was the common language in the first century, and which the inspired writers of the New Testament used in writing. This was also dubbed as the common people or marketplace language.[1] That's why Christ's words were not recorded in oratorical fashion but in words that the mass readers understood that time. Christ even used parables such as The Sower and the Lost Coin, and made several allusions to the relationship of a shepherd and the sheep, because that's what people in almost every level of society would understand.

After preaching in an evening service, one pastor was asked by another worker regarding his secret in delivering a good message. He replied, "Nothing is secret about it, just keep it simple." On another occasion, a pastor was invited to speak in a middle-class church where he preached a simple message on Christ's birth. Present in the crowd was a lawyer who is used to parliamentary, constitutional, and legal terms, who liked how the Word of God was handled and delivered that he ended up inviting the pastor to be one of his regular speakers in his office Bible study. Explaining God's Word in all simplicity is the key to feed & nourish the flock of God. You don't feed the sheep in boxes of grass wrapped in tin foil and bottled water, but you lead them in grassy field and in brooks to drink. What I mean is that you don't need to present the Word in seemingly mystical, oratorical, always-pounding-the-pulpit, or dancing-around-in-a-theatrical-or-comical way, but communicate it clearly in words that are understood by your hearers.

People will flock to a church with professional-sounding music because they have been exposed to live concerts with live bands, smoke and strobe lights. Their focus is now shifted to the performance rather than the message of the song. They have the wrong notion that they feel the Spirit move more if the music is good, not knowing that the essence of spiritual worship is being lost. I am not saying that good and excellent Christian music is wrong, and I can say that being a musician myself, I sometimes push my musicians to their limits because I believe in producing excellent music for the Lord, but not to the extent of drowning the message of the song with fancy music.

Some Christians belittle the music back in their home church because of poor sound system or amateur musicians. They don't see the reality of how expensive high-quality sound system and instruments are and that singers and musicians are only volunteers from the membership of the church. And there are lots of churches who don't allow non-baptized members to be in the music team, further limiting the choices. There was once a church who hired professional choir members to sing in their service. This is an unwise investment of the Lord's money and not acceptable to God. If

---

1. Dana and Mantey, *A Manual Grammar of the Greek New Testament*, 9–10.

there is no one in the church who can pick the right note then do away with the idea of having a choir. Don't be pressured if your neighbor churches or almost all the churches in your group or denomination have one, but focus instead on what you're good at. If you have the friendliest church in your area, then you will be a great in evangelism. If you have the greatest Sunday School program then you will be able to reach many children in your community. If you have an excellent visitation or evangelism team, then you will be able to reach those who are in need in your area. Improve more on what you're good at and use it for the glory of God. Also, some musicians have certain limits with no more room for improvement, and we should learn to make do with them especially when no one else is available. Stop comparing or competing with worldly practitioners because in the church we are not performers but worshippers with God as our audience.

The church cannot compete with the world in terms of conducting our ministry.

First, because in a company, especially in a multi-national one, out of hundreds or perhaps thousands of applicants, they hire the best of the best and pay them according to their value in the company. The hired employees may have transferred from a reputable company, or graduated from the finest universities with good grades, whereas in the church, people with willing hearts volunteer to serve although not necessarily gifted or talented. Although I believe that God calls men and women with the right gifts and talents to every local church because every local church is unique and different from each other according to God's design for every congregation. That's why you should design your ministry according to the kind of people you have and not design your ministry, then fit your people into it. Remember that God calls people to start a ministry and not the other way around. When Christ wanted the world to be evangelized, He called a few ordinary men. He called Saul of Tarsus to reach the Gentiles and He called Aquila and Priscilla to train Apollos. Even in the Old Testament, God called Noah to save the human race, Abraham to build a nation, Moses to deliver Israel out of bondage, David to be a king and all the prophets to their respective ministries. Just like Moses who had only a rod or staff in his hand and a message from God, use what is in your hand and build on that and see how God will display His power through the ministry that He has entrusted to you.

Secondly, companies have the budget to rent or build their own offices, buy the best facilities, advertise, hire expats, or send their people to be trained overseas, whereas most churches just have enough to support their workers, their ministries, and fixed operating expenses. Some churches even need to solicit funds for building repairs and purchase of new equipment. Not all churches have scholarship funds for seminary students who are trained to become future church workers. That's why every church should carefully and wisely use all money that goes into the offering basket or plate. Conduct your ministry modestly within your means. Set your priorities according to your goals and needs. Even if you have the money, it is absurd for you to think of buying a full grand piano during summer when you know that your roof is leaking very badly during rainy days, or your full-time workers are underpaid. You may have a beautiful music, but when it rains you have to put up all your umbrellas to cover your piano and pianist while singing, or that your preachers and teachers will come half-prepared because they have to take a second job to support their families. God knows the needs of your church. Just as He provides for all your needs, He will also provide the needs of your congregation. Do you know why it is that even though God provides abundantly, it always seems to be lacking? It's because you measure God's provisions according to your expectations or your system of counting, forgetting that God is eternal and is not confined in your dimension. You don't see the spiritual blessing that accompanies God's answer to your prayers, and that is to build godly character in you. For instance, if God provides you with just enough, He may want you to learn contentment. If He provides short of what you're asking for, He may want you to trust more. If God does not provide your needs, He may want you to wait or to learn to seek His will. These Godly virtues, once developed in you, are real spiritual blessings that supersede any material blessing that you aspire for because of their eternal value. Be wise and faithful stewards because if God sees your faithfulness in small things, then He can entrust you with greater things.

Thirdly, in terms of worship programs, the church has the tendency to copy worldly entertainment for the reason that they want to attract the people of the world. If you are an unbeliever and are looking for entertainment, you don't need to go to church to be regaled because all you have to do is get your TV remote, sit back, and you have almost a hundred channels from your cable TV to choose from. Someone once unwisely said that "Worship is the key to evangelism." What he meant was that all you have to do is upgrade and produce quality worship service with good music, and unbelievers will come to your church. When Christ called His disciples to become fishers of men, they perfectly understood what they were about to do. They didn't need to be properly groomed, and they didn't need to clean up their boats, paint them with bright colors so that the fish will be attracted and come jumping into the comfort of their properly-decorated boats. But they needed to go out to the sea to catch fish, sometimes in the cold of the night. They may have faced rough weather conditions and sometimes after a tiring overnight labor, they may have come home the following morning with almost nothing in their nets. In the same way, you need to go out and look for lost souls than just wait for them to appear in your church doors. Some would contest about this type of evangelism with the arrival of mega churches, which is the trend of this generation. Let us get this straight, I am not against big churches as long as they promote holy living and preach the Word faithfully, without compromise. Some started small with a few people, started evangelizing without changing their message, and then God blesses them. We praise God for causing them to grow and for rewarding their hard labor. However, some mega churches water down their preaching, don't preach about sin, welcome any religion, and they attract members from smaller churches who are looking for preachers who will tickle their ears.

You can only compete with the world if you stop preaching the true Christ of the Bible and replace it with the christ of your own imagination—one that soothes the fleshly desire of your audience. Because the Christ of the Bible loves righteousness, hates sin, and doesn't teach you how to be materially-rich and free from any kind of trouble or sickness, but He teaches about self-denial, suffering and sacrifice. If you preach the Christ of the Bible, you will be branded as a fanatic, extremist or a lunatic, but it's better to be branded as these than to lose your reward in heaven someday.

Church Example

The church as a corporate body also serves as role model not only to the membership of the Body, particularly to the young ones who will be the next generation of leaders, but also to the outside community. The young people of the church are the silent observers who look up at the older leaders as their role models. If they sense that something is amiss, then they will resent and some may quietly rebel against the older people, creating an unseen gap. Meanwhile, the unbelieving community somehow could also know if there is love and unity in the church or if discord is present. That's why it is important for a church to build a genuine positive image to be effective to

Church Leaders Are Role Models

the outside world, and this all begins with the church leaders. Now let us see some common mistakes churches make and how to correct these:

1. Let's begin with the board members in relation to their pastor. Every time the board members meet and decide how much financial support is to be given to their pastor, he is always excused from a closed door meeting. But what actually transpires in the meeting is an evaluation of the pastor's performance as his support depends on it. And most of the comments are pure allegations which become conclusive. Why not call the pastor into the meeting so that he can answer all accusations? Someone might say, "We don't want to hurt the feelings of our pastor." Don't you think it will be more hurtful for your pastor to know it from a second or third source because by that time he knew that the rumors have already spread around? Do you want to know why you choose a closed door meeting? It's simply because you are afraid to say things to your pastor directly because you are in doubt of the truthfulness of your charges. It hurts, isn't it? I'm not saying that all church leaders have this practice, but those who do, this message is for you. This may sound radical and you might not agree, but know this: no church member is qualified or has the right to evaluate their pastor's performance! Have you seen patients converge to assess how their doctors treat them? If you can understand and define the causes and symptoms of multiple sclerosis, Huntington's disease or sigmoid volvulus then perhaps you can say that you have enough knowledge, but still, that doesn't make you a doctor. Just as only doctors can appraise other doctors, so only pastors can evaluate other pastors since they share the same calling, the same heartbeat, the same passion and experience. They can understand each other in a way which no member can comprehend, and it's sad to think that the most misunderstood member of the Body of Christ is the pastor. But how do you evaluate a pastor? Here are some suggestions: First, let your pastor evaluate himself at least once every three years based on the ministry descriptions that he and the church have agreed upon from the start of his ministry while also considering the goals and objectives of the church. As much as possible, it must be put in writing but not to be shared with anyone from the church. Secondly, if your church association has a committee of pastors to evaluate, then your pastor should meet with them and share his self-evaluation list. If your church doesn't have a committee like that or if your church is

The Anatomy of Church Leaders

an independent one, then your church and your pastor can invite at least two neutral pastors from other churches with the same faith and practice to help in the evaluation process. All church members can share their personal opinions, recommendations or allegations about their pastor, put everything into writing and submit it to the Evaluating Committee in a sealed envelope with their signatures affixed. These are not to be shared with others. Any letter without signature or anonymously written should not be entertained. Then third and last, the pastor must report to the church leaders in a written form the result of the evaluation signed by all committee members. You may not like this or may disagree with this but the committee reserves the right not to divulge everything that transpired in their evaluation meeting. Why is this so? Because there are some things that church members may not understand in the life and ministry of a pastor. The committee must submit a report that may also include commendations of the pastor's accomplishments and strength in the ministry, and mention of some areas in the life and ministries of the pastor that need improvement. Another option is for the committee to just make general statements like "Very Satisfactory," "Satisfactory," "Very Good," "Good," etc., with accompanying explanation of their assessment, and may recommend that the pastor continues his service to the church unless he resigns with corresponding reasons. The pastor with the committee may also decide that he resigns due to very poor performance of his duties. If the latter happens, the church needs to know only the general details and not the specific ones, unless the pastor commits a sin that involves the church and needs to be dealt with. That's the only time that the church, especially the leaders, deserve to know. Treat your pastors with honor and dignity, regardless of the outcome of the evaluation. Always remember that he is still your pastor who is called by God and he needs to be treated with respect and high esteem. He is not your employee, but your spiritual leader. The man may not be perfect and so are most of the men in the Bible as well as all church members. You must love your pastors and treat them kindly, just as you want to be treated. Again, this is just a suggestion of an evaluation process because it will also depend on your church's form of government.

2. We now come to the performance of the ministry. Some leaders in the church (not all churches) have the tendency to have a little competition

with each other and draw attention to themselves. In a wedding that a musician pastor has attended, he immediately noticed a female worker who was about to play the Bridal Chorus. She sat on the piano long before the ceremony started with a straight body and her head unusually held up high. Apparently, she was trying to catch attention as she was always looking around. But when she started playing, the first chord was off and so was the rhythm. It was not even an improvisation because everything was off. If Richard Wagner, the composer, was still alive and present at that time he would probably told her to stop right away. The pastor also wondered why he was not invited to play since he was easily accessible. It was because of competition. The female worker wanted to prove that she is also a good pianist when she is not. She even managed to take a glance at the musician pastor who was sitting right behind her. Just imagine how much she had to stretch her neck just to make sure that he was watching. You may say that the pastor was too judgmental, but he is a seasoned musician and he is familiar with how amateur musicians behave, considering that it was not the first time that it happened. On another occasion, after a disastrous duet number of two young people, he was approached by them right after they sang and asked proudly how they performed. The pastor, being a guest in that event, just politely smiled. He can't even give a proper answer to a performance that is off pitch and can't find the right beat with the accompaniment tape. The music ministry of the church can become a lair for entertainment. Whatever type of church music or instrument you use in your church may become a temptation for some to showcase their musical prowess. Instead of worshipping God and leading the congregation in meaningful worship, some musicians seem to be performing in a concert. There was this lead guitarist who played lead and adlibbed during the whole duration of the song, and a choir member who always sings louder than the others, almost ignoring all the dynamics of the song. It is important to educate and always remind the song leaders, instrumentalists, the choir members and those giving special number to play or sing their parts in unity with the other musicians, and that their role is just to prepare the hearts of the people in listening to the preaching of God's Word, therefore, they must not draw attention to themselves. Some leaders have the tendency to please their pastors, members or other leaders instead of pleasing God alone. In other words, they do theatrical acts instead of doing the ministry.

3. Lastly, we'll discuss how a church advertises itself. While it is not wrong to advertise your church in the television, radio, newspaper or the internet, please don't overdo it. Don't say that you're a caring and praying church when your members are not active in the visitation program and only a handful people attends the prayer meeting. Be honest in what your church can offer and you don't need to hire an advertising consultant to market your church because marketing strategies don't apply to churches. What your church needs is to build a positive image in order to create an impact to your community and eventually to the world. There was a church leader who was known in saying to any brethren who was absent the previous Sunday, "You were missed by everyone last Sunday," when in fact very few people or maybe nobody even noticed the absence of that person. Maybe he was trying to project that their church was a caring church, but their church was well-known for proselyting members from other churches, so it is not wrong to say that the absent member was just a number in their congregation. We are not passing judgment on the leader's intention but a pastor who broke away from this group testified to me the nature of his former church affiliation, and how surrounding churches complained about their proselyting practices.

No leader is perfect in his demeanor, and some leaders fall into the trap of wrong practices without them knowing that they err. We share all these negative examples to you as leaders so that you won't repeat the same mistakes of others who were before you. Another thing to avoid is the tendency of overestimating the number of members in your church when asked. You could end up rounding off to the nearest 50 or 100 of your total membership. When asked by someone it is easy to say, "We have around 50 members," when the actual count is 35, or "We have around 100 members," when the actual count is 82, or "We have around 300 members," when the actual count is 264. We may even include in our count the inactive members. After an evangelistic campaign, some may boast of the hundreds who came forward or prayed to receive Christ but never report how many actually came to church, were baptized and became responsible disciples of the local church. Be not conformed to the world of false advertisement, but be honest and truthful all the time. Remember that you were called to a life of honesty and integrity.

Church Leaders Are Role Models

Contemporary Example

Whether you like it or not, those who are under your God-given ministry look up to you, especially on how you respond to adverse conditions. There is this story of a new pastor who accepted the call of a 60-year-old church and immediately discerned a gap or conflict between the young people and young professionals and the elderly members of the church, particularly the aging retired pastor, who was part of the founding members of that congregation. The youth were disgusted every time the old pastor tells old stories which were repeated again and again for the nth time, because that's simply how old people recount same stories with much eagerness and interest.

On one Sunday, because it was already late, the new pastor decided to forego the Sunday School which was supposed to occur before the worship service. Not knowing that the old pastor, who was sitting at the back, was so furious over the decision of the younger pastor who broke a 60-year-old tradition of having Sunday School first before worship service. After the service, the worship leader asked the old pastor to close in prayer, and then the unexpected happened. As soon as the elderly pastor opened his mouth, he began expressing his resentment towards the situation, and literally reprimanded the younger pastor for his bad call. It was a long discourse that lasted for thirty minutes, before he closed in prayer.

Of course, the young pastor gained the sympathy of the young ones because they knew that the old pastor was unreasonable. Tension was building inside and all eyes were focused on the two pastors as they had to meet on the front door. Will the young rebuke the old or will he just ignore him since he's already too old to be given importance? But contrary to expectations, the young pastor greeted the elderly pastor with a firm handshake and said, "Pastor you were right and I was wrong. I'm so sorry it won't happen again!" That profound statement changed the attitude of the church. First, the old pastor was vindicated and not offended. Secondly, respect for the elders was restored. On the succeeding times that the old pastor would relate his repetitious stories all over again, the young ones have become cheerful, amused and eager to listen, without disgust and dislike anymore. And thirdly, the old pastor, his wife and daughter loved the younger pastor and his family. The younger pastor always visited him on his sickbed and listened to his stories, enabling him to record the details of the church history. It only took three words, "I am sorry," to turn things around. We cannot devalue a good Christian example as it doesn't only heal a broken relationship, but it also shapes the lives of believers. People look at you how you will react when insulted, humiliated or even slandered. If you get angry, fight back or worse, take revenge, most likely they will do the same. But if you show humility at all times and always bring the matter first to God in prayer, then you've set a good example, and you will lead a peace-loving church.

What is heartbreaking is when God's people don't reciprocate to your leadership role. In one of the weekly morning pastor's group devotions, they discussed the experiences and sentiments of some pastors: how they were so eager to visit the sick and help those in need, but in times of their sickness and needs, nobody comes to visit them. In one occasion, a pastor's father in law, who was a member of the church, was hospitalized for more than a week with only the pastor's wife attending to him. Except for an elderly couple, no one visited him to at least pray for him, not even one from the women's group whom the pastor's wife loves and actively participated in. And when the hospital bills came out, the poor pastor was forced to take a loan to pay for the entire amount since no member offered any financial assistance. Another thing that infuriated the pastor's wife was when she asked for prayers for her father in the church members' chatroom, no one even said, "I'll be praying for him," not even one thumbs up. But when one of the members announced the upcoming church outing, most of the members became active again, reacted and chatted back. So out of frustration, she became the first one to leave that chatroom which she herself has created.

Even though the pastor initiates and sees to it that every member who is sick is visited, no one showed up when it's time for the pastor's family to be comforted. You might ask what was in the mind of the members: do they think that their pastor is really strong in faith that he doesn't need comfort? Do you know that there are some members who are blessed when they see their pastor suffering? They are so blessed that they won't even lift a finger to alleviate his hardship. But when it's time for them to suffer, one of the first persons they want to see is their pastor so he could pray for them. It's ironic, isn't it?

One of the horrible things that one of the pastors shared was when a pastor's child died, no one from among the members of the church came to visit during the entire duration of the wake! I just don't know how those members are going to face the Lord on the BEMA judgment. You might think that these stories are parts of a movie scene, but no, these happened in real life.

–7–

Church Leaders Are Consultative

"And David consulted with the captains
of thousands and hundreds, *and* with every leader."

(1 CHR 13:1)

CHURCH LEADERS SHOULD BE wise through God's word, their knowledge about the things around them, and their experiences. But humans as they are, their wisdom is limited so they need to consult with their people. We will be looking at an Old Testament example of consultative leadership, from the greatest King who ever lived, King David of Israel from his story in 1 Chr 13. With David's popularity, he could have easily given the command to return the ark of God from Kirjath–jearim, where the Philistine returned it many years before out of fear of God's wrath. Not only was it God's will to return it but it was also the proper thing to do. But why did David need to consult with the captains and every leader who practically had control over the nation's populace?

Consultation by Following Biblical Example

What is the value of consultative leadership? Here is what we can learn from David:

1. He talked to the leaders only (v.1). By conferring with the captains of the armies he was able to mobilize 30,000 soldiers (2 Sam 6:1). And

by talking to every leader, he was able to gather many people to come with him (1 Chr 13:5). Because it involved the whole nation, he had to consult at least the majority of the people. In the church, we don't need to consult everything to the body. But whenever a decision may affect a group of people, then that group must be consulted or else we might be doing the work alone with nobody backing us up. You must have your core group whom you can delegate the work, and remember that the members of the body have different gifts, and you can assign tasks based on their gifts. Once there was this pastor who had to go out for a one-year Sabbatical leave and appointed a young pastor to handle the church while he's on vacation. The young man, who was overly excited, jumped into the opportunity and literally changed everything in the church building. No, he did not supervise the changes but did the works himself. He redecorated the building, made cut-outs for the letterings of the church theme, and even replanted and repainted the garden. Perhaps if you were his pastor, you will tell him, "Hey young man, you should be studying right now, preparing your sermons and praying. You should not be tending the gardens, leave that to others." They may have a beautiful building but the members were spiritually malnourished because of his lack of sermon preparation. Your leaders are important not only because they will ease your ministry workload, but also through them, you're able to multiply yourself and accomplish more things in the process.

2. He shared his plan to the people (1 Chr 13:2,3). "If *it seem good* unto you, and *that it be* of the LORD our God," (v. 2a). He knew it was God's will to bring the ark back, but He sought the will of God on the proper timing because many years have already passed. In the ministry, it's important to communicate your vision, goals and plan to the whole church through your leaders. If you are the pastor, you can incorporate through your preaching or teachings. If you are a lay leader, you can mention it to your members every time you meet. Although this could be difficult if you have leaders or members who are always antagonistic towards you, and most likely won't cooperate and will just sit on the sidelines watching and waiting for you to mess up. These members or leaders are likewise armed with their canons of criticism, and will begin to open fire on you at the smallest chance they see. You need to deal with them personally by applying the suggestions in Chapter 5 of this book under the heading, "Motivation

Church Leaders Are Consultative

by Personal Dealing." Now it's not only the "what" and "how" that must be considered but also the "when." Are the people ready for the undertaking? Is there enough budget to begin with? If it is a long-term project, it must be sustainable. If it is a short-term project, then even the month or season of the year must be considered. That's why we need to consult our people not only for their support, but also for their wisdom and ideas. There is a proper time to execute God's will. Take the analogy from a marriage union. Although you're convinced that the person with you is your future spouse, you don't just go to a minister to perform your marriage ceremony anytime you want to. Both your parents may like you to become husband and wife, or you may have been best friends since childhood, or the whole church has been praying for you for a long time, but still, that doesn't mean that you can plunge into marriage anytime you wish to. You have to consider and do first the following items:

a. You must pray to God for the right time, especially for the man's proposal to the woman.

b. In some culture or family tradition, the man must formally ask the woman's hand from her parents or family members no matter how old they are.

c. You must prayerfully plan for your married life-where you will live, how to handle your finances, who works and who doesn't, how many children you're planning to have, and all other complicated and simple matters like how to divide the household chores, the schedule of buying groceries, and where to put the shoes and used socks upon arriving at home. These may seem trivial to you but these simple matters can become the source of irritation that can turn into a major quarrel. These may not be the sources of anger between you but these simple matters may become the trigger to a fight that may lead you to court. An old pastor who used to advise married couple always says, "Continue courting each other and you will stay out of court." As you can see, it's not just the planning for the wedding ceremony that is to be considered but also the post-ceremony itself or how to live your married life together.

d. You must decide whether it's a big or small, private or close family wedding. You must make the necessary reservation of all the wedding suppliers that you need, including the availability of the wedding and reception venue. Don't hesitate to go back to your drawing table if you can't find a suitable venue that is available on your target wedding date, taking into consideration the possible availability of the participants.

e. You must set the date of the wedding when all the participants will be available. You must be able to communicate with all the members of the entourage and wait for each response, and that may take time.

f. You have to secure the necessary legal documents.

g. You have to undergo pre-marital counselling with a pastor who will decide the duration and how often the counseling will be.

h. And other details like appointment with the officiating minister, getting the right wedding coordinator, applying for leave from work, honeymoon and regularly checking the progress of the preparation. The wedding ceremony will only last for an hour or two, but the preparation, consultation and getting of advice will take a longer time. So there is a perfect time to fulfill the will of God and that is when everything and everyone is ready. Again, the right time of executing God's will is essential especially in the context of the church since it involves many lives.

3. The whole assembly agreed and David began to move (vv.4,5). We are used to hearing about the need for a majority vote for any decision that we make, but in the church, it should always be a unanimous vote especially in major decisions. Everyone should agree to guarantee full support of the Body. We can only apply majority voting in minor choices such as what food should be served during the anniversary, what color of curtains should be purchased, or what week of the month are you going to have your special fellowship. The problem with majority voting is that not all will be supportive, and that the majority is not always right as is the case of the twelve spies (Num 13:1—14:45) sent to Canaan, wherein only Joshua and Caleb believed that they can conquer the land with God on their side but the other ten said "No!" So it was a majority vote of ten against two. Then later on, the ten influenced at least the adult citizens of the entire nation. Meanwhile, with Joshua and Caleb were Moses and Aaron who fell on

Church Leaders Are Consultative

their face towards the assembly of the people, or perhaps to all the leaders of the tribes, or to all those twenty years old and above. At that time, it was an overwhelming majority with a whole nation against four men. And the story might have ended with these four men's death had not God intervened for them and punished all those who opposed by death. We can see clearly from this story that the majority is not always right and this also applies even in the church, especially if most of the members don't walk in the Holy Spirit. Even though opposition may come only from a few people, these few people have a way of manipulating or magnifying things. They will say things like, "You know many say that . . . ," when only a handful say that or the statement comes from them alone and they don't want to admit it. Or, "Everybody complains that . . . ," when only a minority group actually complains. When that happens, just calmly ask, "May I know who these people are so that I can talk to each one of them personally?" If what they're saying is true, then they will give you a list of names, and you can make an appointment to have a dialogue with each of them. If it is not true then they might say, "Err . . . Brother so and so and Sister so and so said that . . . ," (excluding themselves), ". . . and many more others!" Then respond by saying, "Can you please provide me the names of those 'many more others'?" Take out a pen and paper and have them list names with their own handwriting under the heading "Complainants" or something like that, write the date and have them sign their names below. If they can't do that they will probably say, "We can't do that because we promise not to reveal them. It's confidential." How can such a thing be confidential if it is already a public knowledge? Just politely say, "I'm sorry but I can't entertain your complaints unless you give me their names." Just a word of precaution: don't ever suggest that you want to meet with all the complainants in a group meeting because they can bring in a lot of people who have no knowledge of the accusation or have no idea why they are in that meeting in the first place, and they will only come to know once the issue has been laid before them. How many times did we hear some of our members say, "I didn't know that there is an issue like that!" It's good if many, if not all, don't believe them and still side with you, but if many people believe them, then it will be bad for you because you only accumulated more critics, and your litigant will say, "See, there's your 'many more others'!" How can such people do things like that?

The Anatomy of Church Leaders

It's because some people believe that they are the voice of the majority. That's why consecrated lives is a must especially for the leaders so that all will be in tune with God's will and right decisions can be made. Otherwise, those who voted in the negative might say, "See I told you so!" whenever a problem arises, and this might cause division. Since there is only one will of God, then everyone must agree so that when problem comes, everyone will surely participate in the solution. But what if one or two strongly disagree with everyone? Not all who disagree are talking nonsense, some are reasonable and factual in their opinions and worth listening to especially if you know that everyone in the group is walking in obedience in the Lord. Having different opinions has nothing to do with spirituality, but with background, experiences and frame of thinking. Some are objective, while others are subjective; some are practical, some are technical, while others are emotional in their approach to decision making. There are different ways and different angles to resolve any issue, that's why all perspectives must be explored especially on concerns that are not specified in the Bible. There is also a chance that those in the negative are right especially if they are more knowledgeable and experienced on the matter at hand. If this is the case, you must postpone your decision and listen to their arguments carefully, and as a group, you must find a solution until adjustment is made and everyone can agree. Once during a church board meeting there was a heated argument because the members wanted to discuss some problems that involved several members of the board. Only the pastor opposed the idea because emotion was so high at that time, and this might further lead to more heated debate with no conclusive resolution. Secondly, he didn't want to shame anybody as it will produce more anger and perhaps division among the leaders. The pastor held his ground and succeeded when he promised to talk privately to anyone who has concern. When all emotion has died down, no one bothered to talk about it anymore and it has been forgotten. Had the pastor allowed it to happen, it would have erupted and might have caused much damage in the church. Now if it can't really be avoided, after all options to reconcile are exhausted, and there is really a need for a majority vote, then those in the minority or negative side must learn to respect the decision of the majority. They must support the judgment of the many and must not resort to murmuring or criticizing, and must refrain from

Church Leaders Are Consultative

propagating their views to others. This is not easy because of their human nature to wish that it will fail, that's why more maturity and spirituality are required. Once, the leaders of a small group of churches convened to discuss an ethical issue to be implemented to all their churches. Since the Bible is silent on the issue, there was a long discussion on the subject matter until a conclusion was made by the group. Everyone agreed except for a leader who disagreed based on his understanding of the Holy Scripture. Then the leaders called all the members of their churches and discussed with them the decision that was made on the ethical issue, and made everyone agree. Most of the leaders spoke and answered the questions by some members. Before the meeting concluded, the lone opposition leader raised his hand and asked for permission to speak. Most of the leaders were so worried that he would voice out his opposing view. But when he started to talk he simply offered a funny yet truthful suggestion should an ethical situation arise in the church. All the leaders were relieved, and in fact nobody in the group knew that he opposed the leader's view, because he was mature enough to respect the majority's decision. As a postscript for this story, the time came for a situation where the concluded ethical standard made by the leaders will be put to test. It turned out that many of the church leaders and members did not follow the ethical decision they made but they went the other way, thus revealing their disagreement with the early decision of their leaders. The leaders were silenced and could not do anything about it. Had they considered the opposing view of the lone leader, they could have avoided putting themselves in an awkward position. On the part of the mature opposing leader, not even a word of "I told you so," or blaming others or pointing finger came out from him. This is what "respecting the majority" means, you must support the body whether you are right or wrong, unless it is a major doctrinal error, or condoning of sin, or the leaders are becoming a stumbling block to the members. In such cases, you must prayerfully rebuke the leaders of your church. If they listen to you and they stop from their sinful ways, then it is good. But if they don't want to listen and change their ways, then you must come out and resign from that church and look for another church that teaches the right doctrine and promotes holy living.

The Anatomy of Church Leaders

Consultation by Seeking God's Will

God's will could be classified into two aspects: the first is His Divine or direct will and the second is His permissive will.

First, let us consider the Divine or direct will of God. God can speak to you in various ways like using someone who talks to you directly, the natural circumstances of your life, or past experiences. But the best tool from which we can derive God's determination is the Bible itself, God's written words. Some are directly stated and some are derived from the principles it teaches us. But be very careful in claiming a promise in the Bible because some are written for a very specific audience and time, and it may not be for you. Take for example Acts 16:31 where it says "And they said, Believe on the Lord Jesus Christ, and thou shalt be saved, and thy house." Many Christians believe that all their loved ones, especially the first degree relatives will be saved even if they were not able to witness to them personally. But upon looking closer at it, you will find that this verse was spoken by the Apostle Paul with Silas at that time specifically to the Philippian Jailer when he asked Paul how to be saved. It was a statement made unto him and not a promise to everyone. How do we know that? Through the verse's grammatical construction. The words from this verse "Believe, thou (you), saved and thy (your)' in the original Greek language are all in the second person singular, which means it refers to the Philippian jailer. Some may argue that of course he was talking to a man that's why he used words that is singular in form. But take a look at John 3:7, "Marvel not that I said unto thee, Ye must be born again." Jesus was talking to Nicodemus alone one night that's why Christ used the pronoun "thee (you)" in the second person singular form, but the next pronoun "Ye (you)" is in the second person plural which means that it was not only Nicodemus who needs to be born from above to enter the Kingdom of God, but everyone. It is a little confusing in the English language because "you" can mean singular or plural depending on the context of the speaker unlike in the Greek language of the New Testament time where it is always specified according to its usage, and in Acts 16:31 it refers only to one person. Then there is the doctrinal side of it, which means that the salvation of the soul is personal and it has nothing to do with your family. There is nothing such as corporate solidarity when it comes to becoming a child of God, especially during this church age. So as Christian leaders, it is imperative that you study the Word of God carefully so that you may know God's will and be able to help others. When the

Church Leaders Are Consultative

Bible is not specific on some matters that need action, you may use these principles that were shared by a certain pastor years ago:

1. The Principle of Ownership (1 Cor 6:19-20) "Whose owner are you?"

    Your body and life now belong to God. Therefore you must be very careful on how to use your body. If you borrow a car from someone (not a car rental), you will be very careful in driving it and you'll have it washed, and fill the gas tank before returning it with no scratch or dent. More so with how we use our bodies that belong to the Lord. In 1 Cor 6:18, the Apostle Paul spoke of fleeing fornication that began in v. 15. The command "flee" in the Greek is in the present tense which signifies a continuous or repeated action, which further tells us that fleeing is a struggle that we have to face on a daily basis. To flee is not an act of cowardice, but of gallantry. At one point during the Korean War in the 50's, around 12,000 American troops were trapped at Chosin Reservoir in North Korea with the sudden attack of the armies of the People's Republic of China, aiding the depleting North Korean Army.[1] They were surrounded and outnumbered on every side, casualties were growing in number on a daily basis, and they were on the verge of annihilation. Then they received orders that they should go back south to safety. That didn't mean that they were surrendering, as General Oliver P. Smith said, "We're not retreating, we're just advancing in a different direction."[2] It's always wise to fall back when lives are at stake and so we should advance to the rear if there is a threat to fall into temptation. The Apostle Paul was talking about sexual purity both in our minds and body. We are living in a promiscuous time in our society where free sex is advertised in the movies, books, magazine or the internet, and where a radio announcer called it normal for single couples to do. But the children of God must be different, single people must maintain their chastity and wait until they get married to the right person. My advice to single men is to respect the ladies and treat them as your own sisters. And to single ladies, don't let any men touch your bodies or take advantage of you and avoid these kinds of boys or men. By touch, I'm referring to the erotic kind of touch by the opposite sex. If you're a Christian, and you commit this sin, you will regret it for the rest of your life because you've lost something

---

1. AmericanExperiencePBS, "Chapter 1 The Battle of Chosin."
2. Wikipedia, "Oliver P. Smith."

that you can never take back. Sexual purity is true not only for single people but also for married ones. In Heb 13:4a, the writer of the book said, "Marriage is held in honor, and the bed is not defiled." Married people should remain faithful to their spouses. When you signed your marriage contract it is not renewable after 2, 5 or 10 years, but it is meant for life. Again, my advice to any single Christian out there is do not take anybody to be your boyfriend or girlfriend just for the sake of having a partner, unless you plan to marry that person. Enjoy your single life, you don't need someone to be by your side always, and you have your friends and brethren in the church. You can actually be close with a Christian from the opposite sex provided that you have mutual respect for each other. Enjoy your godly freedom as a single person, it comes only once in your life until the time that God Himself will lead you to the right person and you say your "I do." Here is a funny quote I wrote and shared in my Facebook account:

> Remember it's not 'for bitter or for worse,'
> But it's 'for better or for worse.'
> It's not 'in sickness or bad health,'
> But it's 'in sickness or good health.'
> It's not 'Until debt do us part,'
> But it's 'Until death do us part.'
> And when the Minister asks, say 'I do,'
> And not 'Do I?'

2. The Principle of Influence (Rom 14:13) "How will it affect the brethren?"

Will your action promote encouragement to the Body of Christ or will you become a stumbling block especially to the weaker members? Not all Christians share the same convictions in all matters of life. Different churches have different cultures and traditions too that you must learn to respect. These differences are not only in matters of the type of music, clothing, length of hair (both for men and women), but also in practices. There is a Christian church where women wear veil on their heads, so if you're a lady believer who plans to visit that church, you should bring and wear your own veil so that you will not become a stumbling block especially to the new believers in that church. So before making any decision in life, always consider what the local body of Christ that you belong to approves or disapproves. The Apostle Paul reminded the Corinthian believers, "But take heed

Church Leaders Are Consultative

lest by any means this liberty of yours become a stumbling block to them that are weak." (1 Cor 8:9). You have the liberty to choose what you want to do with your life, what to wear, what to eat or where to go. Remember that you live in a Christian community and not all may share your preferences especially if these may cause them to stumble. For instance, you choose to work in a bar and this doesn't affect you at all because you are not a drunkard. But what if you have a brother in the Lord whose family and career was ruined because of alcoholism? Will it not affect him, especially if you're a known leader in the church? It's either he will think that it's okay for him to go back to the bar too and once he smells alcohol again he may not be able to resist going back to drinking, or he may judge and be angry at you. In either occasion, he sins against the Lord. A seminary professor once told a story of a man who hated saxophone so much because he was once a sax player in several nightclubs where his life took a plunge before the Lord saved him. So in this case, it's best if his church will never consider using a saxophone in their worship service. You must never use your Christian liberty to gratify yourself alone but consider others who may be weak in certain areas of life.

3. The Principle of Glorifying God (1 Cor 10:31; Col 3:17,23) "Does it give honor to God?"

    This is a major question that you must answer before doing anything. The chief purpose of every Christian is to glorify God. Everything that you do must be for the glory of God. It's not us who should be exalted. Don't think that you are glorifying God just because you feel good about it. Your own greatest pleasure in life is not the gauge of a God-glorifying activity, but the principles from the Bible are. Some Christians think that church hopping is good because by going from one church to another and as they listen to different preachers every Sunday, they think they are growing in their relationship with God. They compare attending church to eating in different restaurants where they must try something new once they get bored with the same menu. But even with this analogy, you would notice that more mature and stable people would go and hang in the same diner or restaurant almost every day, would order the same kind of food or are excited to try something new in the menu, and know almost every service crew by name. In the same way, God is more honored if you stay in one church where the spiritual nutrition is balanced through the systematic preaching of your pastor, through the different ministries where you can serve, and through fellowships where you can find people to support and pray for you. And if you are in trouble, you have your own pastor to call, which is almost impossible if you're just a church hopper and a stranger to almost all the churches you've visited. Think of your church as your home, where you have a healthy family, and parents who provide for all your needs until such time that you can already make it on your own, and siblings to play and confide with when you are in trouble. And when you grow old and move away to have your own family, you will find it a joyous occasion to visit home once in a while so that your kids can visit their grandparents and hear the stories of your childhood and family history. You will be glad to be back in your own room enjoying the familiar smell of everything. But if you are a church hopper, where do you think you will bring your kids and what do you tell them about your home church? Remember also that your church is your training ground for your future ministry or vocation. I have seen many successful pastors, Christian workers, and professionals attended Sunday school and stayed in one church at least in their early years. So if you want to glorify God aside from having your daily devotion to begin with, love your local church, stay with it and serve through it until the Lord leads you to move to another location that is relatively far from your former residence. In everything you do, always align yourself with the principles of the Word of God or seek advice from more mature Christians to ensure that you are living a God-honoring life.

4. The Principle of Redeeming the Time (Eph 5:16) "Will it waste your precious time?"

    An opportunity wasted cannot be retrieved anymore. God has given every person 24 hours daily to live, and how you spend each precious minute will be accounted for. There is a time to rest, and a time to work or study, there is a time to serve God, a time to spend with friends for leisure, and a time to be alone with God. It's better to set a daily goal on what you want to accomplish for the day and set it as on top of your to do list whether it's in the morning, afternoon or evening. Look forward to accomplishing it, and be fruitful and wise in spending your remaining time of the day. Perhaps you have experienced coming home very tired and wondered what have you accomplished that day. The term multi-tasking only applies to few

Church Leaders Are Consultative

people who are highly trained on a given time. They may be a simple housewife who is cleaning the kitchen and at the same time listening to the weather forecast while cooking the food. Or an office clerk who has to answer an important phone call and remember important details while rushing to finish a work on the computer, with the boss yelling out instructions. Or an air force pilot on a combat mission who maneuvers the plane, checking on the flight control panel and radar for any approaching enemy plane and noting their positions, watching for any missiles coming at them while aiming or firing a gun on enemy planes and at the same time listening on their headset for instruction. But for most of us, we could only focus on one task at a given time, so we must focus on something important at least for the day. As an old saying from an unknown author goes, "'If a task has once begun, never leave it till it's done. Be the labor great or small, do it well or not at all."[3] Never be distracted and finish well what you are doing unless an emergency comes up that needs your full attention.

5. The Principle of Companionship (Ps 1:1; 2 Cor 6:14) "Will it mean to compromise or fellowship with unbelievers?"

   By fellowship I mean doing the same evil things that the unbelievers do. Sometimes temptation comes in the guise of opportunity which may lead you to a trap of a compromising life. Once you're in the snare, then it may be hard if not almost impossible to get out. Beware of those who offer you easy comfort or easy money because you might end up penniless or worse, in jail. Be careful with whom you are dealing with, otherwise, you may be travelling in the same road downhill. If you're invited to go to a place where you know or even have the suspicion that temptations abound, never even take the risk to go there. It's easier to say no before you leave than when you are already there at the forbidden place. It's easier to say no than fall on the first time, and then on the second time, and fall again the hardest on the third time. The more you fall, the more you drift away until you're at the bottom of the valley. At this time you may think that God is already too far away to be reached or even to hear you. The truth is God knows exactly where you are and if you're a true believer in Christ, the Holy Spirit will never leave you and is still silently working in you but you can't hear or notice Him because it's you who distanced yourself from God. You can always come back to Him, admit all your sins and

---

3. Banks, "If a Task Has Once Begun, Never Leave It Till It's Done."

ask for His grace to restore you back. Remember Paul's command in 1 Cor 15:33, "Be not deceived: evil communications corrupt good manners." It doesn't mean that we stop being friends with unbelievers because they need to see Christ through us, but avoid those whom you think will influence you more than you can influence them.

6. The Principle of Growth and Maturity (2 Pet 3:18; Phil 3:12–14; Heb 12:1–3) "Will it contribute to your spiritual growth and maturity?"

   Will your decision help you come closer to God or will it lead you away from God? A young man was offered a job in a leading company but his position requires him to report even on Sundays, preventing him to attend Sunday service in his church. He turned down the offer and settled for a job with lesser pay, but won't entail him to work on Sundays. For him, nurturing his relationship with his God is far more important than a high-paying job. If your walk with God, spiritual growth and maturity are most important to you, then it will define every move you make. But in cases wherein economic situations entail you to accept a job that requires you to work on Sundays, then find a way where you can worship God regularly. In a certain place, there was a church that has their Sunday Worship Service start at four o'clock in the morning because most of their peoples' work starts at six o'clock in the morning, some work late in the afternoon, and some in the evening. Also in some countries, churches don't hold their Worship Service on Sundays, but during weekdays depending on the religious culture of the state. One of the most common questions of young professionals today is "How can I know if God wants me to work in the place where I am right now?" To begin with, ask yourself, "Am I growing in my spiritual life or am I slowly declining in my current job?" "Am I becoming stronger in my trust and obedience to God's Word or am I gradually living a life of compromise?" The spiritual things should be your primary concern, and the physical comes in second, such as the issue on salary, distance, the workplace and physical fatigue which may be damaging to your health. The physical concerns can be given solution but you cannot bargain for the spiritual benefits that you get from your present job. However, if there is no more remedy to the physical situation because of the reality of your needs and failing health, then you can pray for another job, because God has promised to provide all your needs and wants us to be healthy always. Although sickness will surely come, it doesn't need to be self-inflicted.

Church Leaders Are Consultative

Secondly, let us consider the permissive will of God. We use the word "permissive" to discuss the point here. Sometimes, God directs His will but you are already settled in your mind on what to do. You may use the term "seeking God's will" to justify your position and you may look for verses to take out of context just to fit your will into God's will, and may seek advice from your likeminded friends. God sometimes intervenes through circumstances in life, just like a strong storm which came on the wedding day of a Christian lady and an unbeliever, yet she persisted in disobeying God. Also, there was this young Christian girl who is a daughter of a widow, who got pregnant by an unbeliever, claiming that they are in love with each other. When the boy asked the girl's hand in marriage, the girls' mother refused. The girl rebelled against her mother but somehow, the mother's decision prevailed until the daughter gave birth to a baby girl. The mother's reason was simple, "You have committed a mistake by getting pregnant out of wedlock. Don't make a second mistake by marrying an unbeliever." The principled widow stood by the Word of God. Besides, the girl was still young and there is a chance that she could find a Christian man who will love and accept her and her child. But the girl was too stubborn that after a couple of years she eloped with her ex-lover, the father of her child, and they got married. After a couple more years, the man left her and their child. Now she's alone and doesn't have the chance to find a real Christian man because she's still married to him and she lives in a country where divorce is not allowed by law.

Sometimes, God allows you to do what you want, in spite of His prodding and revealing of His will through His Word, and lets you suffer the consequence. Sometimes the consequence is light and temporary, while sometimes it leaves a permanent scar on you. Although God might have forgiven and forgotten your sins (Heb 8:12; 10:17), but because we live among regenerate and unregenerate people, some people may never forget what you've done, your ministry in the church may be limited to some extent, or the laws of your land might prohibit you from doing some things, just like the girl who eloped in our story above. But consequences may also be beneficial because it keeps you humble and more watchful and vigilant. Some say that you have settled for the second best, but there is only one best and that is to be at the center of God's will. If God knows that you're making a wrong choice, why does he allow you to go through it since He is sovereign? One night, during a Bible study in a home of a Christian family, the light suddenly went out. The mother of the house lighted a few candles and placed it at the center table. When she turned her back, her young son was overwhelmed by the flickering fire, began moving towards it, and touched it as his father silently watched him. As soon as the boy's forefinger touched the fire, he immediately backed off and cried. Then the Pastor asked the father, "Why did you just watch your son touch the fire, knowing that it's dangerous?" The father calmly replied, "You see, it's the first time that he saw a fire, and he doesn't know its danger yet, so I let him touch it under my watchful eyes so that he'll know what it means to play with fire. Next time he won't play with it anymore." Going back to our question above on why God allows you to go with your wrong choice, remember that God always warns you if you're making a wrong turn. The warning can be through His Word, through human beings, through your own experience, through natural circumstances, or most importantly, through the Holy Spirit. But if you continue to keep a deaf ear or turn your face from Him, then He will allow you to wallow in your own folly. So it is for you to experience, know and understand the consequences of disobeying His will for your life. A certain pastor has this leadership style: He will tell you what to do, and when you disagree and insist your own proposition, he will let you have your own way. And when you realized along the way that you were wrong, he will ask you to come back to him, to talk it over again and correct the situation. Why is it that the pastor does not insist his own way, knowing that it is the right thing to do, and doing otherwise may mean a waste of time and resources? Because the pastor knows that he can only motivate, offer suggestion, and can't force anyone to obey him. Besides, he will only allow you to have your way if it is not a direct violation of God's Word, or if the foreseen damage will be tolerable. You might obey out of compulsion but you lose the joy of serving God. But, if you learn from your own mistake, then you will learn to submit to your leader next time, and your pastor has earned his respect from you. This only applies on a personal level and it's a different story when a group is involved.

Consultation by Seeking Advice

It is always good for leaders to have their own mentor. If you can't find one, have your own support group. A mentor is someone who is more spiritually mature, although not necessarily in physical age, more experienced, and more knowledgeable than you. A support group is a group of people who shares some common things and their level of spiritual maturity is not far

Church Leaders Are Consultative

from each other. There are three reasons why you need to find these people. First is for advice, second is for guidance, and third is for accountability.

1. For advice–Never be ashamed to admit to yourself and to others that there are things that you do not know, and don't be surprised either if your pastor says that he doesn't know the answer to your question. That's the reason why we need to seek advice from godly people. There's always wisdom in looking at godly experiences of people who had walked the same road that you are trekking now. It helps that you become aware of sharp stones, what to do on steep climbs, and being careful on downhill travel. Once a family was travelling on a SUV van with a built-in GPS (this was the time when GPS in a vehicle was still new in the market). At one point, because of the traffic, one of the passengers suggested to the driver that they take a U-turn and take another route instead of going straight as the computer suggested. As soon as they turned, the computer began protesting and said something like "You're heading the opposite direction, turn back" or "stay on the right and climb on the ramp then go back." This was repeated for several times to the amusement of the family. When they were nearing their destination, they began driving through a maze of smaller streets and the computer became silent. The next thing they remembered it saying was "destination reached." When the driver was asked how he knew where to pass through the maze of roads, he simply said, "I grew up in this place." He must have passed those roads more than a hundred times already so he knew the way better than the artificial intelligence of a car computer. And so, a more experienced godly person is the best source of information.

2. For guidance–In our journey through life we need at least someone to guide our way. Although God's Word is enough for us, there are still lots of possible distractions that may hinder or delay our travel. Just as road signs are placed in strategic places to be easily seen by travelers, and a lighthouse is very important to sea wayfarers especially during stormy nights, so Christians who are full of wisdom as human guides are just as important. Sometimes in our spiritual travel we can be lured in entertaining sweet-talking people, causing us to be delayed in our arrival to our destination. Or we may chase a beautiful stray cat until we lose our way back, or get busy texting with our cellular phone until we fall into a manhole. The sweet-talking people, the cat and

texting represent temptations, difficulties or problems that may take away our focus, so it is always good to have someone or a group of trusted people to remind us that we are travelling through the wrong lane, or that we are making the wrong turn or heading to a ditch. Some good Christians have the ability to look at the whole picture of life, just like an airplane pilot or a drone plane on a reconnaissance mission who knows where the enemies are positioned and where their troops can pass safely. Some, however, are like the vehicle drivers who need constant instruction from the plane hovering above lest they end up on a dead end, a blown-up bridge, or worse, fall on an enemy ambush. Most Christians have limited vision ahead of them because God designed us to walk by faith and not by sight (2 Cor 5:7), and so, sound guidance from godly people is precious in your life's journey.

3. For accountability–Although our ultimate accountability is to God and nothing is hidden from Him, we still need people to give account to. These are the people that God uses to remind us of our duties to Him and to fellow human beings. One area in life that we need to be accountable to is the area of temptation. If you know that there is temptation right before you and you know that deep in your heart there is a possibility that you can succumb to it, please be honest and don't keep it to yourself. Tell it to someone whom you can confide to, may it be your leader, your mentor or your support group. These are the right people who can protect and warn you if they think you're leaning closer towards the enticement. Don't ever think that you're strong enough to withstand the trial. The Apostle Paul gave his warning during the 1st century A.D., "Wherefore let him that thinketh he standeth take heed lest he fall." (1 Cor 10:12). While this warning is true during the early church, it is still true up to this day. So be accountable to God, to yourself and to others.

One pastor who is the head of the ministry and doesn't have anyone to report to decides to record his daily activities, first for himself so that he can see to it that no single day is wasted and secondly, to share it with people within the leadership, for the purpose of accountability. As I've said above, our ultimate accountability is to God, but it's always wise to also be accountable to our fellow human beings.

Church Leaders Are Consultative

Consultation by Listening to Others' Ideas

A church leader is a good listener and consults the members before making any decision. All church leaders are fallible and although they may have a doctors' degree, that is only limited to their field of expertise. One summer, a newly-graduate high school boy who had two years of elective subject in automotive mechanic decided to take a crash course in diesel engine trouble shooting and maintenance where most of his classmates were older than him and mostly professionals. One day as he entered the laboratory room he noticed his three classmates who were having a small conference among themselves as they were gazing at a car battery in front of them. One was a mechanical engineer, the other was an electrical engineer, and the third was a civil engineer. Noticing their confused faces, as though they were in deep trouble, he asked them what the problem is, and one of them said, "We are discussing amongst ourselves whether this battery is fully charged or not." Without thinking, the boy picked up a battery cable lying around and pressed one end to the negative terminal and scratched the other end to the positive terminal bringing a strong bluish spark, and said, "There, it is fully charged." The three men appeared confounded, asked him, "That's it?" He replied, "Yes, that's how you test a battery!" The three engineers might have been discussing theories and were taught that car batteries are made up of plates facing each other, divided into compartments, adding a mixture of electrolyte and distilled water, enclosed in a rubber or plastic casing with the two terminals protruding, but they were never taught how to test the battery voltage without the aid of a multimeter tester.

Sometimes this thing happens in the church, where leaders spend wasted hours in endless meetings, planning and figuring out what to do without asking for opinions from the experts. Some have this proud idea that leaders should know it all, while others are too embarrassed to ask others thinking that they will lose their respect, but actually, the opposite happens. People will lose their respect for you if you pretend you know something but in fact, do not. On your first, second or third move, an expert will easily recognize if you really know what you're doing. Have you ever watched a comedy movie where an actor pretends to know karate because he's going to fight a real fighter, and makes this funny fighting stance and this weird Bruce Lee sound? And the next thing that the actor remembers is getting punched in the face? Well, that's how you look like in front of experts without you consulting them. You might be heading on a hit or

The Anatomy of Church Leaders

miss, or trial and error path which might mean losing precious time and church resources.

There is this story of a pastor, and a church member who was a lawyer. The lawyer was a studious student of the Bible and can even memorize the names of the kings of Israel and Judah in proper order. But every time there is a difficult passage he encounters in the Bible, he asks his pastor. The pastor on the other hand, doesn't pretend to know everything that involves legal matters and calls his lawyer friend to seek for advice. Even if the pastor is much younger than his friend, their friendship goes a long way and they both have a mutual respect for each other.

There's also this story of a self-made young worker who was about play the keyboard to accompany the singing in a youth fellowship, who went to practice before the fellowship starts. At one point in the song, he could not find the right chord, and no matter what keys he pressed, he cannot find the right combination. After frantically trying several times, he left disappointed. But his misery could have been alleviated if he just asked the musician standing next to him. That musician knows all the chords in the book and even those not in the book, which means that if you press any combination of keys, he could give it a name. But he was not consulted, as the young worker was too proud to ask. As mentioned above, good church leaders should not be ashamed to admit their limitations but be humble enough to consult even those people under them. Again, the Body is composed of many members with diverse spiritual gifts, talents, experiences and specialization in their respective fields, and so leaders must recognize each ones' capabilities in order for the church to function like a finely-tuned engine. An engine is composed of many parts, from the main engine block to the smallest screw, and each one is designed for a specific purpose. If you dismantle each part separately, you will notice small holes in some engine parts. Those holes were not drilled there for decoration but for oil to pass through in order to lubricate some moving parts of the engine to prevent friction that might cause an engine breakdown. Some parts are twisted or bent just at the right angle not for it to look more beautiful, but in order for it to fit exactly where it should be. Some of these parts are made of hard metal, some of rubber, and some of plastic designed and placed exactly where they are needed. And when they are put together according to their proper place, with the correct pressure on some bolts that have to be tightened and exact clearances on some gaps, adding fuel and motor oil with the correct specified viscosity, then the engine will run smoothly, silently and

Church Leaders Are Consultative

with minimal vibration. So the members of the church are placed exactly where they are with all their strength and weaknesses because God has a purpose for each of them. The good news is that church leaders don't need to hire consultants, but just need to ask some members who may have the experience and knowledge on certain fields.

– 8 –

Church Leaders Are Respect Earners

"And we beseech you, brethren, to know them which labour among you,
and are over you in the Lord, and admonish you;"

(1 THESS 5:12)

In the English Bible, the verse started with the conjunction "And" (Greek-*de*) and is used as a transitional or continuative particle that can be translated "moreover, then or now,"[1] and is used to introduce a new section of exhortation after Paul spoke about the second coming of Christ (1 Thess 4:13—5:11). There are several topics for his exhortation on this last section of his letter and the first subject is about how we should deal with our church leaders.

Together with Silas and Timothy, they requested them to respect (Greek-*eidow*) or "to have regard, cherish, pay attention"[2] to their spiritual leaders especially the pastors. Not only because it was God who placed them in position, but also because Paul gave three good reasons why we should respect our pastors.

---

1. Dana and Mantey, *A Manual Grammar of the Greek New Testament*, 244.
2. Thayer, *Thayer's Greek Definitions*.

Church Leaders Are Respect Earners

They Earn Respect Because of Their Labor

Pastors labor among you. The word "labor" here pertains to the idea of working to the point of exhaustion. Faithful pastors are heard preaching for about forty minutes to one hour every Sunday but few people know how much time, effort and labor are poured in just to make one sermon. Even with the advent of computer and the internet, the work of sermon preparation hasn't been made easier, as technology only speeds up finding information. The preacher still needs to read the Bible several times, check on the grammar, look up the meaning of words in their original language, read articles on Bible cultures and Bible lands, and sometimes watch hours of Biblical and historical documentaries to get their facts straight on the illustrations they will use. Add to that the gathering of information from the local news in order to know what's happening in the economy, politics and religious arena in the world today. You might have heard of pastors who suffered heart attacks or being burned out. At the time of this writing, there is an announcement in a social media group account asking for prayer for a pastor who is confined in an ICU, and in comatose state due to septic shock. And the other month, a pastor sadly relayed how three of his colleagues passed away due to heart failure. One was 50 years old, the other one was 53, and the third one was only 55 years old, and were relatively young at the time of their death. I just don't know if it was ministry-related but as mentioned earlier, some pastors don't complain if they feel something wrong in their bodies simply because they don't want to stop doing the ministry. They know about their great responsibility in the church and they work hard to the point of exhaustion, and for others, exhaustion becomes fatal. And it is sad to think that most members are insensitive to the physical and spiritual condition of their pastors. They always think of them as paid employees who have more day-offs than working days. To think that most faithful pastors are working hard but are under paid. I'm not talking about rich tele-evangelists with mega-churches who preach a watered-down gospel for fear of losing their members, but regular faithful pastors who preach a true and complete gospel.

A certain pastor has the habit of recording his daily accomplishments for personal accountability. If you'll take a peek of his schedule, you'll find that he starts at 8:00 in the morning and retire at about midnight. You will also notice that his one day-off per week is sometimes filled with other activities.

The Anatomy of Church Leaders

A faithful pastor spends a minimum of sixteen hours just to prepare a sermon. That's about half day every day, while others spend more time. Then he has to attend to some paper works like writing correspondences, editing the bulletin program for Sunday, reviewing church policies plus preparing devotions or messages for special services or Bible studies. He has to visit some members, do counseling work, his phone is always available 24/7 and is reachable by members anytime for emergencies. Some pastors retire at around 1:00 or 2:00 a.m. and has to wake up at 5:00 a.m., and they don't receive any overtime pay. Instead, some are paid with criticism by some unsatisfied members. It's maybe because they only see their pastor preaching for an average of one hour on Sunday and maybe another hour on weekday service, and they think that's all the pastor does. Only two hours of work and he gets paid a lot! What about the remaining 166 hours of the week? Maybe sleeping until noon and waking up in time for lunch, then take another two hours of nap, then spend the rest of the afternoon watching movies on YouTube. After dinner, he watches television until he fell asleep on the couch with the remote control dropping from his hand dreaming, what's for lunch the following day. But on Sunday morning, he has to wake up earlier because he has to prepare the message he got from the internet. This may be an exaggeration and I am not saying that there are no lazy pastors, but the point is that faithful Pastors work hard and are willing to give up their rights, and sacrifice everything for the flock of God. These are the qualities that some members don't see in their faithful pastors. A group of young people one time woke up their pastor and asked him to drive them to another town at 2:00 in the morning. They were not aware that the pastor had a heart problem and he needs enough rest.

That's why Paul, even centuries before, told the Thessalonian believers to give regard to their leaders because he had already observed how pastors pushed themselves to the limit, serving the Lord through His people. My advice to church leaders is to get enough rest and take that much needed vacation, because the work never ends. Don't be like the pastor who never used his vacation for about eight years, perhaps for fear that the church will be in chaos if he will be gone for a few weeks. It is understandable if you are pastoring a new church or if a church is in its pioneering stage and you haven't train leaders yet, but it's a different story if you're in a established church. Another thing is learn to say no if you discern that the invitation can be put off to another day or time. If you want to stay long in the ministry, stay strong and healthy by taking enough rest. And members should realize that their pastor also need time to rest or have time with his family. If it's not a pressing concern, try not to bother your pastor during his weekly day off or in the evening when he is with his family. Pastors have their limitations too and can be subjected to being stressed or burned out.

They Earn Respect Because of Their Care

Pastors care for you. The participle "are over" (Greek-*proistaymee*) does not only mean a presider, but also as "guardians and protectors."[3] They are spiritual leaders who watch over your souls and spiritual life. They are responsible for praying for each member, and ensuring that their needs are met by the church. The inflected Greek form of this word (Greek-*proistamenous*) is in the middle voice (not active or passive). The Greek middle voice has no exact equivalent or representation in the English language. But the idea gives us two possible meanings:

a. It may mean calling, with special emphasis given to the subject or the doer of the action which is the spiritual leader. It gives importance to the position and ministry of the spiritual leader. If this is what the writers wanted to convey, then they wanted to call attention to the special roles of the pastors in the church. That's why in verse 13 Paul said, "And to esteem them very highly in love for of their work's sake." This passage admonishes us that our pastors and spiritual leaders should have a special place in our hearts. Note that Paul's admonishment to love is not based on their strength and weaknesses in the ministry but in consideration of their work and labor as mentioned in number one above. Although all Pastors can do all that is needed in the ministry, not all pastors are great preachers and teachers, not all are great administrators, not all are great in discipleship or evangelism, but all faithful pastors work hard that's why we should love them. Appreciating your pastors once in a while will be a great encouragement to them, although well-meaning pastors don't seek that and a simple "thank you" for their labor may already mean a lot to them. Remember that "rewards are given in heaven, but appreciations are made here on earth." When someone says, "That was a great sermon, Pastor!" it may be a little bit confusing to the pastor, because it might mean that the person might have only been entertained by funny illustrations which

3. Thayer, *Thayer's Greek Definitions*.

may be the only thing that is remembered by most members. Or it may mean that the person was deeply wounded by the double-edged sword that is the Word of God. The pastor cares for you and doesn't want to hurt your feelings but he doesn't back down when it comes to preaching against sin, and faithfully communicates it to God's people. It may inflict wound upon your soul but that's because he loves and cares for you and doesn't want you to go wayward but wants you to walk the straight path of God. Reciprocate that love because he's your pastor who cares for you.

b. It may also mean that the doer participates in the result of the action. So it means not only the leaders who should protect and guard the spiritual life of the members, but also the members who should do the same to their pastor or leaders. You must take care of your pastors. Protect them from gossipers, backbiters and slanderers. Pray for them and their families. One of the tragic things that occur in some churches is that when members can't find any fault in their pastor, they lock in to the pastor's wife or children as the main course in their conversations, hoping that they can attack the pastor. Surely your pastor would appreciate it if you tell him directly and privately any concerns that you have about him. People who have no courage to confront their pastors but resort to gossiping or talking behind the back are either not sure if their accusation is factual, or they may feel that they are better or holier than their pastor. One pastor was deeply hurt when some members laughed and talked about another, younger pastor in front of him. They were laughing not because the young pastor was funny but because of his immaturity, which was a false accusation. He may be young, but he was not immature and knows his Bible well than most of them combined.

I still can't comprehend why there are some people in the church who don't have the guts to confront the pastors and instead resort to an evil practice of backstabbing. Just like what happened in a church, as they were having their scheduled weekly Bible study that was being led by the pastor. Then there was this leader who scheduled another Bible study in the house of another member at the exact time as the church's Bible study. Isn't that pure rebellion? When the patient pastor later on enquired about the Bible study topic from some who attended the house meeting, they said that they discussed nothing, and the only topics that they discussed were his (the pastor's) flaws, incompetence and unlikely characteristics which, upon close examination, was 95 percent false. Having known the pastor, I am not saying that the pastor was totally faultless. But 5 percent was only a trivial thing compared to the 95 percent accusation.

If that happened during the Old Testament times, then that wayward leader could have ended up a leper and thrown outside the camp if the Lord didn't opt for that person to be swallowed up by the ground or became a sumptuous breakfast for hungry lions. Brethren, to go up against your pastor or any spiritual leader is purely a hateful matter to God and don't wait for Him to discipline you. There was this powerful deacon in a church who was vehemently opposed to their pastor that he wanted him out of the church. So he set a meeting on one Sunday to formally terminate the services of the pastor. But on the eve before the meeting, his son got involved in a terrible car accident. It was then that the deacon and the members realized that no one should go up against God and His called servants.

Please don't disrespect your pastor but give him importance because he genuinely cares for you. Don't be like this member who just purchased a brand new van and upon reaching the church, saw the pastor's old vehicle parked in front. He then asked his pastor to remove his car and park elsewhere because he's going to take that parking spot for his new van. The pastor was kind enough to remove his old car to give way to his members' new van. Perhaps you would angrily say, "Who gives this person the right to eject the pastor from a parking space that rightfully belongs to him, just because he has a new vehicle?" But can't you see how some pastors would be willing to give up their rights because they care for you? Some would just quietly walk away and pretend that they haven't heard others talking behind their backs although it hurts so much. Some would just keep quiet in spite of the injustices done to them and just leave the matter to God in prayer. Some pastors' children couldn't understand why their respective fathers would not defend themselves, and many young people are not encouraged to enter the ministry because they have silently observed how the older people of the church treated their pastors, although those who are truly called end up in the ministry just the same.

They Earn Respect Because of Their Admonition

Pastors admonish you. The word "admonish" means "to exhort" with the idea of warning, to caution or reprove gently. Being the spiritual father, it is expected that pastors are the most knowledgeable with the Bible so they can discern if something is amiss in someone's life, even before the concerned person becomes aware of it. To some pastors, the hardest part in their ministry is to correct erring brethren. It hurts to see a member do wrong and commit sin. It also hurts the pastor to reprove someone and sadly, pastors are sometimes misunderstood for their loving action and wrongfully judged. How many of you actually thought that when your pastor preaches about a certain sin, he is directing his message to you because you only just might have been guilty? It's either you humble yourselves before God and be willing to be corrected, or be proud and unwilling to accept correction and then try to get back at your pastor.

Good pastors will not customize or design their message to zero-in on someone or a on a group of people in the congregation. In fact, most pastors will not address an issue through the pulpit if someone is involved in the church but will take some other time to confront the brethren involved. We can call a pastor a coward if he uses the pulpit to throw all his accusations against anybody in the church, simply because preaching is monologue and the other party will not be given the chance to air his/her side. There was a pastor who was preaching one Sunday morning and saw a lady member coming in late. As the lady was entering the worship hall, he looked at her and suddenly mentioned about the "sin of coming late to church!" The poor lady was totally embarrassed and was already judged without hearing her side. Some preachers get too excited while preaching that they utter side comments without considering their audience, and in the end, make fools out of themselves. Some would quote a verse and forget the next phrase and invent their own words. Some abuse their authority, thinking that they have all the right to say anything under the appearance of being led by the Holy Spirit. And some would tell impromptu illustrations that hurt some members or forget how the story would have ended. One Sunday morning, a pastor was preaching and a story came into his mind. Without thinking twice, he suddenly told a story of a young woman who got pregnant and left by his boyfriend. And as he ended up his story, he happened to look at the face of a Christian lady guest who got pregnant and left by his boyfriend and was known by everyone in the audience. Although he was referring to another person, the preacher quickly realized the mistake that he just made. The reason why that lady was attending their church was that she found love and acceptance from the church members, but this foolish story by the preacher came out of nowhere and appeared as though he was condemning her. The pastor bowed down his head in total shame as though a bucket of ice cold water was poured all over him. He almost lost track of his sermon and didn't know what to say next. If only he could run away and hide, he would have done so.

Some older and experienced pastors can see a problem miles away before it even hits home. That's why they preach, warn the brethren or make church policies to address future issues. Some pastors have the ability to see what's in your heart by how you answer them. A simple way to illustrate this is when a pastor asked a young man if he can accompany him on a funeral service in another town. The young man answered, "That's too far!" The pastor knew right away that he was not interested. If he was, he would have asked "What time are we leaving?" Or "What do we need to bring?" It's like asking someone to jump from a staircase and get a reply, "From what step?" And not "Why do I need to jump?" Because a willing person does not ask "why?" but "how?"

Notice also that the word "beseech" (Greek-*erowtowmen*) is not in the imperative (command) mood but in the indicative which is a simple statement of fact.[4] Paul and company simply entreated the Thessalonian believers to respect their spiritual leaders. In Rom 13:1, Paul commanded the Roman believers to be in subjection to the government authorities. It was a command because every civilian had no choice but to submit to the government, and any violation would result to punishment. But it's so much different in the spiritual Body of Christ, because you can't command the members to respect you, rather, you have to earn it. We don't like people to respect us because they're afraid of us or because of our position in the church. But we want to be respected out of mutual agape love for each other.

It's also important for leaders to nurture their relationship with their members. And a good relationship starts with a healthy communication. At first there is only acquaintanceship, where you might only know them by name, where they work, who are their family members and any public information about them that can be easily obtained from others. You might be able to talk to them occasionally or casually after Sunday Service, after mid-week service or whenever you happen to bump with them in a grocery store or somewhere else. Seize every opportunity to engage in a meaningful conversation even for a few minutes. You can begin by asking them how they are doing. There are some people who never were asked that question, they may be a teenager, a housewife, a common laborer, a manager, or even

---

4. Thayer, *Thayer's Greek Definitions*.

The Anatomy of Church Leaders

a CEO in a company. Ask them about their family or work, and if you sense that there is something that you can pray about them, tell them that you will pray for them. And when you part ways don't put off the prayer at a later time, because there's a chance that you might forget about it. As you are walking away from them, say your sincere prayer. It doesn't need to be a long one but an earnest supplication will do. The next time you meet, try to inquire about the last item that you prayed about them. Say, "How was your exam, Johnny?" (Always call them by their first name). Or, "Hi Susan, how's your sick daughter?" Or say, "Mark, have you met that deadline at work last Friday?" Try to recall names, dates or occasions. This will show them that you are really interested in them, that you are listening, and that you mean every word you say. There was this young worker who was conducting a home Bible Study when four young girls were invited to join them. After a casual introduction of each of them, they began their Bible Study. Then in the middle of the discussion, something unexpected happened. The young worker called each girl by name, who then giggled and whispered loudly to each other with big smile on their faces saying, "He remembered all of our names!" It's not that because the young worker was relatively handsome that's why they giggled, but because they felt that they were important in the group. And so he got their attention until the end of the study session. Again, a good relationship starts with a healthy communication. You can be funny or cheerful in your initial conversation with them, but the most important thing is that you leave a godly impression on them.

Some homegrown Bible school students or newly graduate pastors struggle for respect when people of the church call them in their first names instead of addressing them "Pastor." The members saw them when they were still young boys running around and they are used to calling them in their first or nicknames. These young workers have some misconception about respect because they think that it is associated with their titles. When people call you "Johnny, Danny, Tommy, etc.," even though you're the senior pastor, chief deacon, a doctor or a company CEO, it is not a sign of disrespect, but a term of endearment especially by people who are close to you. So my advice for young workers is this: people will eventually call you "Pastor" if they see that you begin to act as one, and see in you a true Shepherd's heart. It took twenty-five years for a certain pastor to be ordained in the ministry for the simple reason that he doesn't want to be called "Reverend" because he sees that title belongs only to God, and we respect him for his view in this matter. He only submitted himself into ordination when it became a government requirement.

So respect is not dependent on title, your educational attainment or social status, but on your character which speaks of who you are. What people see in you will determine your respectability. If you ask people to respect you, most probably the opposite will happen—you will lose it. Seek for more spiritual maturity, watch how you act and talk. I am not saying that you should always be serious in dealing with others and stop being funny sometimes, but a person with a godly character, even in his/her humor, you will be edified. A 21-year-old young man who is a believer for four years was elected as a board member of their church. Fresh out of college, he worked as the part-time caretaker of their church. Aside from another young man, the other members of the board were all accomplished professionals who were all in their middle age, and two elderly men. Being young, he is still sometimes playful and acts silly, but he earned the respect of the congregation because of his spiritual maturity, and his manner and speech. At his young age, he is already leading Bible studies to fathers, heads of the family, and the elderly. He does not struggle as most young preachers do in preaching or teaching the Word of God to much older people and he doesn't remember being too nervous while speaking before a crowd no matter how small or large, because he is confident in the God he represents.

For people to respect you in the church, be respectable and act respectable. It's not because of your title or position that you are respected, but it's because of your confidence in God, your life and conversation that make people respect you. Church leaders earn respect from members and not command them to give respect. Respectable leaders would be listened to and be able to control waning ministry situation because people have confidence in them.

Before we close this chapter, let me offer you some practical advice on how to handle unlikely circumstances in the church, that you may earn respect from among God's people. I've said earlier that, "Some older and experienced pastors can see a problem miles away before it even hits home." It is always important to have a plan B if in case something mild or worse happens. Take this real-life scenarios: it's a wedding day of a pastor and the officiating minister did not arrive, what would you do? You have a scheduled guest speaker but did not come, or what will happen to a church when out of miscommunication or lack of proper coordination, two prominent guest speakers arrived to speak? And out of respect for each other, both speakers walked away. What would you do? Or in worse scenarios, a pastor suddenly had a heart attack or a group of four pastors from different local churches of the same denomination died in a car crash, leaving four churches orphaned. How you respond to situations like these will define your leadership respectability.

Of course, we can't predict the future for any eventuality so we must somehow be prepared and take necessary steps to have mental notes of what to do. Take some of these examples: a pastor is known for scribbling down at least a rough outline of the text assigned to all guest speakers in case they don't show up. One Sunday morning, as the service has just begun, a member requested his pastor who was the speaker that morning to come with him because his brother-in-law was dying and he needed to be witnessed to. So the pastor called the most mature male member of their congregation and asked him to preach that morning. This shows the importance of having a detailed outline for others to follow in the event that you suddenly become unavailable. Then there was also this pastor whose cousin, who belonged and used to be active in another religious group, passed away. Every night, there was a mass by nuns and their layman. On the night before the burial day, as the pastor and his family were heading home, he asked himself, "Is there a chance that I would be asked to lead the committal ceremony at the cemetery?" He did not dismiss the idea altogether but gave a 1 percent possibility because of the presence of many religious leaders from the first night of the wake, and surely until the burial. This was the same pastor who was mentioned on the chapter on prayer who panicked when he was called to lead the service on the cemetery years before and forgot everything to say so he just prayed. That was how he learned the lesson to be always prepared. So on their way home he began a mental note and began memorizing the message he is about to share. After a few hours upon reaching home, the wife of the deceased called and asked him if he could lead the service at the cemetery, to which he gladly said yes. So the 1 percent possibility became a 100 percent reality. The following day, he was able to speak without notes, except for the Scripture reading, from the opening prayer to the short sermon and the committal itself. That's what I mean by having a Plan B, to be always prepared even on remote possibilities. Always anticipate what might happen. When you go to a family, clan or class reunion, and they know that you are a Christian, most likely you will be asked to lead in prayer or give some words of encouragement. If you're a pastor or a male leader in a city church and you happen to visit a small

Church Leaders Are Respect Earners

town church, it is wise for you to bring with you your Bible and sermon manuscripts of your old sermon. Because there is a chance that you will be asked to exhort in one of their services in a moment's notice by their pastor. This is especially true if that church is seldom visited by others from outside their town. For them it is an honor to have you as their speaker and for their pastor to sit down and be ministered to especially if he's the one who faithfully preaches week after week. While this is true in small town churches, this also applies to big city churches. Once there was a foreign pastor who visited a city in the United States and attended a home Bible Study conducted by a pastor from that city. It was the first time that the two pastors met and after engaging in a meaningful conversation, the visiting pastor was asked if he could speak on the coming Sunday morning service, which he gladly accepted.

Although we are not superstitious people and we don't believe in luck because everything that happens to us is within the confines of God's will, still, you should not live carelessly and be responsible for your own safety. You might not agree with this but it is advisable for two pastors of the same church not to board the same plane together or ride the same car together especially in long trips. If there is only one car available, let the other pastor take the back seat. So that in case of accident, one of you will be safe. I am not saying that we can prevent God's will to happen, but the point is that even though God's will shall surely come to pass, we are still responsible for our own safety. For example, you are a sixty-year-old person and you have a heart problem so you are taking your maintenance medicine. Your doctor forbids you to eat certain kinds of food, but you still eat them anyway because your philosophy is "If I perish, I'll perish." Let's say the Lord calls you home when you're seventy (of course we don't know that), so you have ten more years to live. If you live with the kind of mentality mentioned above, you may not be able to live a quality life for the next ten years because you may be bound in a wheel chair, unable to move and talk coherently. Remember, God will surely protect us, but we must also keep ourselves safe always.

Epilogue

SINCE THE CHURCH IS one body, holy in position, but composed of diverse kinds of human beings who sometimes walk in the flesh and not in the Spirit, it is therefore susceptible to all kinds of problems. And some of these problems are not external but are caused internally. The leaders play a major role either in the cause or solution to the troubles inside. As we all know, there is no such thing as a perfect or trouble-free church, but most of these problems can be eliminated or avoided, if only the leaders will humbly obey the Lord and walk in the Spirit always.

First, be sure that all the leaders of your church are called by God in their respected places in the ministry and that they are with the right spirit, right attitude and right spiritual gifts. This may be difficult in cases where the whole congregation has to choose, nominate and elect their leaders, especially the board members. In some churches, the most influential, most popular, most vocal, or the ones who belong to the biggest clan in the church are elected although they are not supposed to be in the leadership position because of spirituality, maturity, and attitude problems. This can be eliminated by making some alteration in the process which can be done by giving pastors the authority to prayerfully select the nominees to ensure that all who will be chosen are qualified to become leaders. Then out of the chosen nominees, the congregation may elect or vote for the leaders. Another option is the creation of a committee which is composed of spiritual, mature and unbiased members of the congregation to select the nominees. Although this is not a guarantee of a problem-free leadership, but at least the potential biggest problem is eliminated.

Secondly, the leaders should have some degree of Bible knowledge and doctrines. They should have regular personal daily devotions and a continuous hunger for the Word of God. Christians are like airplane pilots who need to always be in constant communication with the control tower.

Epilogue

Although they have the on-board computers to fly a plane, they still need the tower to guide them on the runway during take-off and landing and even while on the air. The control tower could also sense if the aircraft is in trouble and communicates with the pilots if they are flying off-course or maneuvering on the wrong altitude. The Word of God is like that as it guides us since the day that we began our spiritual journey until we land in glory. That's why it is important for us to contemplate on the Holy Scriptures to give us daily direction.

Thirdly, the leaders should have a God-given burden to pray for their members, leaders and the lost souls on a regular basis. No Christian would ever grow in their faith apart from God's Word and prayer. While God speaks to us through the Written Word, we speak to God through prayer, thus, forming a healthy communication with our Lord which can result to a sure spiritual growth. Since God knows everything about us, praying to Him therefore shows how much we trust and rely on Him on everything that transpires in our lives.

Fourthly, the leaders should have a servant attitude, knowing that their God-given position in the church is just their role that is to be used in serving our One and only Master, our Lord Jesus Christ. The pastors, deacons or any member of the board are not the boss, but are all servants of the Lord Jesus Christ. God placed them in their respective posts so that everything in the church can be done decently and in order.

Fifthly, the leaders should exhort and encourage each member to obey the Lord and do their parts in the ministry. By using the Word of God, they should be able to motivate and make an appeal to the reasoning, create a need in their heart, and make a decision to heed to the instruction of the Bible.

Sixth, the leaders should always set a good example to the body of Christ. It is said that in any learning process, it is "easier caught than taught." This means that the people of God can learn humility by example, if they can see it exemplified in the lives of the church leaders. A young Christian is so eager to learn the Bible that he always accompanies his pastor in conducting home Bible studies, quietly observing how the pastor patiently explains Bible truths and tactfully answers questions. After several months, his pastor asked him to lead a Bible Study in a family of new converts, and he did great on his first try as though he was a professional Bible teacher! All he did was study the lesson and emulate the gentle teaching of his pastor.

The Anatomy of Church Leaders

Seventh, church leaders should be humble enough to seek advice from their members and learn to accept any brighter ideas than theirs. Consultative leaders always refer the matter at hand especially to the people who will be directly affected by the decision to be made. You may have more knowledge in spiritual things, but don't be surprised if some of your members are more knowledgeable than you in technical, legal or even practical issues in life.

And lastly, leaders earn respect and don't command or ask people to give it to them. Certainly you don't want your members to follow you out of fear, or out of the notion that God will punish them if they disobey you, out of compulsion, or because of your position. Rather, you want them to follow you because they love God and because they love and respect you as their God-given leader.

God called and appointed leaders in their respective ministries so that each member will be guided accordingly. The victory or failure of a ministry starts with the leader, knowing the fact that we have an enemy who always aims for chaos in the church leadership. Therefore, all church leaders must always unite and have the same mind, same heart and same purpose, which is to glorify God in everything they do.

More than three decades ago, a young Bible school student received an anonymous call from a lady who was a member of a big city church. She said that she was sent by her church to talk to him regarding their intent to call him as their new pastor. What was odd about this call was that he never met anyone of them yet, have never seen their church congregation, and none of the church members has seen him before either. He was only known as a good preacher and the youngest pastor in a generation of pastors. When he said that he cannot accept the call since he is still in school, the lady on the other line said it doesn't matter because they believe that it is God's will for him to be their new pastor. He then sensed that the lady or her church will not take no for an answer, as she narrated the benefits that he will receive, which was very tempting, and insisted that he pack up his things already. The lady was very persistent and the young man seemed to run out of excuses. But he found a break in their conversation when the lady said, "Pastor, the Lord told us that you will be our new pastor." Gathering his last ounce of reasoning he calmly replied, "Ma'am, now I'm convinced that it is not me that you're looking for, because if the Lord told you that I'm the one, the problem is that God has not told me about it. I'm so sorry that I can't come with you." The lady was stunned, then she

Epilogue

stopped from her long discourse. The young worker didn't want to take part in a church with leaders who have poor discernment and poor decision making. Therefore, leaders should always seek to grow in an intimate relationship with our Lord, develop godly character, and do everything for the glory of God alone. They should always exercise sound judgment in all that they say and do and always consider it a privilege to be called in the ministry, serving the King of Kings and Lord of Lords.

The grace of our Lord Jesus Christ be with you as you pursue excellence in serving Him alone.

Bibliography

AmericanExperiencePBS. "Chapter 1 The Battle of Chosin." *YouTube* video, 9:37. October 25, 2016. https://www.youtube.com/watch?v=zYfWhb_YNEA&has_verified=1.

Banks, Melvin. "If A Task Has Once Begun, Never Leave It Till It's Done." Urban Faith. https://urbanfaith.com/2016/10/task-begun-never-leave-till-done.html/.

Brown, et al. *Brown-Driver-Briggs' Hebrew Definition*. Franklin, TN: e-Sword 7.7.7. https://e-sword.net.

Dana, H.E., and Julius R. Mantey. *A Manual Grammar of the Greek New Testament*. Toronto, ON: The Macmillan Company, 1927.

Gill, John. *Gill's Exposition of the Entire Bible*. Franklin, TN: e-Sword 7.7.7. https://e-sword.net.

IsraelinPH. "Thank You Philippines (Part ½)." *Youtube* video, 31:56. October 12, 2015. https://www.youtube.com/watch?v=IFCTgIAGHHI.

Keil, Karl Fredreich and Franz Delitzsch. *Keil and Delitzsch Commentary on the Old Testament*. Franklin, TN: e-Sword 7.7.7. https://e-sword.net.

Mitchell-Gosa, Carolyn. "Definition and Importance of Motivation." Motivation is Fundamental. https://motivationisfundamental.blogspot.com/p/motivation-relationship-to-learning.html.

Swindoll, Chuck. *Insight for Living*. Far East Broadcasting Company. Metro Manila, Philippines: FEBC: 1980s.

Thayer, Joseph Henry. *Thayer's Greek Definitions*. Franklin, TN: e-Sword 7.7.7. https://e-sword.net.

Wikipedia. "Oliver P. Smith." Last modified February 18, 2020. https://en.wikipedia.org/wiki/Oliver_P._Smith.

www.ingramcontent.com/pod-product-compliance
Lightning Source LLC
Chambersburg PA
CBHW072147160426
43197CB00012B/2275